T0207571

Walk Steadfast

On the Promises of God

Sarah N. Vaughn

WESTBOW
PRESS®
A DIVISION OF THOMAS NELSON
& ZONDERVAN

WestBow Press books may be ordered through booksellers or by contacting:

WestBow Press
A Division of Thomas Nelson & Zondervan
1663 Liberty Drive
Bloomington, IN 47403
www.westbowpress.com
844-714-3454

Because of the dynamic nature of the Internet, any web addresses or
links contained in this book may have changed since publication and
may no longer be valid. The views expressed in this work are solely those
of the author and do not necessarily reflect the views of the publisher,
and the publisher hereby disclaims any responsibility for them.

Any people depicted in stock imagery provided by Getty Images are models,
and such images are being used for illustrative purposes only.
Certain stock imagery © Getty Images.

ISBN: 978-1-6642-0992-3 (sc)
ISBN: 978-1-6642-0991-6 (e)

Library of Congress Control Number: 2020920719

Print information available on the last page.

WestBow Press rev. date: 11/12/2020

To you, the reader,
May this book give you hope and strength
to walk into your miracle.

CONTENTS

INTRODUCTION

In a society that glorifies instant gratification and quick results, most have lost the ability to remain steadfast. Steadfastness is key to seeing the promises of God fulfilled in our lives. When running a race, runners have two options: choose to quit or choose to keep going and finish. They may not *feel* up to the challenge, but they're determined to see the prize at the finish line. The good news is that what matters most is not what we feel like doing; it's about what we've determined in our hearts to do. Let's determine to discover God's promises!

As for me, my faith journey right now is as "simple" as walking. *Walking*—the act of putting one foot in front of the other, an act resulting in moving from one place to another. This was an action that was said to be *impossible* for me. I was told at the age of two that I would never be able to walk without assistance.

> It had been difficult to believe the day before *the day*. The day after *the day*, it was impossible *not* to believe.
> —Mark Batterson, *The Circle Maker*[1]

My first "the day" moment happened when I was five. I was in kindergarten, and I had a wonderful teacher—Mr. Collins. He believed in me, and for some reason that made me believe in myself. One day, on the way to lunch, he made me walk down the hallway by myself. I remember crying, thinking it was impossible. I had always relied on other people or my crutches. I had never known what it was like to walk freely.

With a friend close by, I took my first steps. Crying and afraid, I did it. That five-year-old girl did it! What was pronounced as an impossibility, I accomplished! But not on my own. I had the support of my teacher, my friend, and, most importantly, God. I could not have done it without God.

As I got older, I always wondered about a phrase I saw on posters at school. It read, "All I really need to know I learned in kindergarten." (Robert Fulghum[2]).

That phrase stuck with me. I believed there was truth in that statement, but that the truth I take away from it would be different from what others take away from it.

Then, one day, in worship, the Lord revealed to me what I had wondered for so long. What was the truth in that statement for me? Why had it resonated with me?

> Jesus replied, "What is impossible with man is possible with God." (Luke 18:27 NIV)

"Nothing is impossible with God" is a fundamental truth that I learned in kindergarten, and that is what my faith believes even now—with God all things are possible.

Let's dive into His truth together. There are things yet to come that may have been pronounced as impossible in your life, and I am writing to tell you they are not!

Building on the Foundation

> The strong spirit of a man sustains him
> in bodily pain or trouble, but a weak and
> broken spirit who can raise up or bear?
> —Proverbs 18:14 (AMPC)

The key to steadfast living is training our spirits to be strong. A strong spirit of a man sustains us. "Sustain" in this verse is the Hebrew word *kuwl*, which means "to maintain, abide, bear, hold, and provide sustenance."[3] Our spirit is the most important thing to keep strong because it can provide us with an oasis in times of pain or trouble, if nourished.

> You will keep in perfect peace those
> whose minds are steadfast, because they
> trust in you. (Isaiah 26:3 NIV)

Those whose minds are steadfast can also be translated as *"those whose minds cannot be changed," "whose minds are stayed on You,"* and *"people who maintain their faith."* Because the Lord has graciously helped me maintain my faith in times of bodily pain and trouble, I have learned how to strengthen my spirit and overcome barriers to see the impossible become possible in my life.

I want to let you in on the truths that have launched me into my destiny. You may not be aiming to walk *literally*, but we're all aiming for something! And, if you're not, I believe that you will aim for new dreams, goals, and possibilities with much inspiration after reading the words contained in this book. The Lord prompted me to write this book so that you can begin to walk and move into His realities of promise. That's not a typo. God's promises are more of a *reality* in your life than your current circumstance or struggle.

God has so many promises for you! Will you take a walk with me? Let's move into your promised land.

PART ONE ▬▬▬▬

Overcoming Obstacles

— ONE —

The Steadfast Spirit

One day Jesus told his disciples a story to show that they should always pray and never give up.

—Luke 18:1 (NLT)

The days following "the day" in kindergarten were not all rosy. I still had many challenges to face and many obstacles to overcome. Despite the fact that I had the freedom to take a few steps, I still had to rely on my crutches to assist me in walking. I used them at all times in public. But at home, I would attempt to walk without them. I desperately wanted to experience more mobility growing up. But progress rarely comes easily in anything.

Impossibility tries to grip everyone at one time or another. Facing struggles and adversity for an extended period alters the thought process. What limits you will attempt to become the loudest influence defining you. It's important to use your authority and decide who or what defines you.

As for me, I refuse to let disability define me. It won't

name or label me. A name is what we're known by, and my true identity is in who I am—Sarah, God's princess. I'm known as an overcoming child of God.

Impossibility will not only fight to be a big influence on you, but it also has a good chance of being your native language if you let it. It's time for you to learn a new default language.

Possibility.

Determination.

Steadfastness.

I can.

I will.

All things are possible with my God by my side.

Relentless Ruth

When I want something—when I cover something in prayer—my heart is set. I desire God's will, and as a friend of God, sometimes there's a no-question-about-it advantage. Sometimes we just know what are our friends' wishes, likes/dislikes, wants/needs, and interests without asking. We know them. We don't have to ask, "This one or this one?" We know their preferences. The same thing can happen in our relationship with God. Because of our time spent in His presence and in His Word, we have a no-question-about-it advantage on some things.

God reassures my heart when there's more He has for me. I sense God's hand of favor on a certain desire or thing, and it stirs my faith. I experience an immovable determination to see a promise fulfilled. My heart is set. A heart set is a heart steadfast.

Ruth is the first person in the Bible recorded as steadfast. Her heart was set to go with Naomi. Ruth could have had a very different story if she had chosen to allow herself to be swallowed up in grief at the loss of her husband. However, Ruth has a great story of hope and redemption. Ruth didn't stop in her pit of grief. She realized she had nothing to cling to from her past.

Her former life was no more, but she felt so connected to her mother-in-law, Naomi, that she couldn't bear the thought of leaving her. Ruth saw something in Naomi. She saw faith in the midst of bitterness and despair; she saw a devotion to the Lord. Ruth begged her mother-in-law to let her stay.

> But Ruth replied, "Don't ask me to leave you and turn back. Wherever you go, I will go; wherever you live, I will live. Your people will be my people, and your God will be my God." (Ruth 1:16 NLT)

Ruth wanted to honor Naomi by staying with her. There was an investment in their relationship built up over the last decade that she refused to abandon. Ruth's statement to Naomi made her intentions clear. When Ruth declared that nothing would separate them, Naomi took notice of Ruth's steadfast mind. "When she saw that she was steadfastly minded to go with her, then she left speaking unto her" (Ruth 1:18 KJV). The Message paraphrases it like this: "When Naomi saw that Ruth had her heart set on going with her, she gave in." Naomi stopped urging Ruth to turn back after realizing how serious she was. Ruth ended up being pretty amazingly blessed after this steadfast decision! It was not a coincidence. Ruth was blessed for her determination, her devotion to God, and her unrelenting obedience.

Ruth was not simply the first woman to be recorded in God's Word as steadfast; she was the first *person* to be recorded as steadfast in all of God's Word! Ruth obtained so much favor with the Lord just by remaining persistent! You are invited to join in on many blessings and promises as well if you walk steadfastly.

What God Sees

God doesn't discriminate based on gender, race, appearance, or ability. He looks at the heart (see 1 Samuel 16:7). When God looks at me, He doesn't see my weaknesses and limitations. He sees the beautiful, strong spirit He created. He sees me covered in the righteousness that Jesus brings. And He sees the magnitude of what He has created in you as well! He smiles when He looks at you. From personal experience, I like to say that God laughs with us too. Oftentimes I get elated when I do the simplest things. It's just amazing to do the impossible. And when I find God gracing me yet again with such opportunities, I just explode in joy; I almost can't help it. Sometimes I hold the joy in because no one else would understand. Some things only God knows. Only God knows the deepest cries—or laughs—of our hearts, and only God can respond in a way that settles our souls. He touches hearts in an instant as only He can do.

I find it ironic and at times irritating that Sarah, Abraham's wife, was known for her laughter. We constantly hear the perspective that she laughed at the possibility of the promise because it seemed improbable. And God called her out on it! God most certainly will have something to say about my laughter when we meet face-to-face as well. I wonder if she, like me, also laughed in joy after the fulfillment of her promise. Can you picture her filled with uncontainable joy after the one she waited twenty-five years for finally arrived? What a glorious moment to hold a promise in your hands and not just in your heart!

Heart Substance

What is the promise that takes up the most room in your heart? What do you pray about the most? Where is your heart set? What do you want to see? It's important to visualize these answers because you're going to set off on your journey soon. (We'll talk about that in part 2 of this book.) But unlike us, the Lord can see the whole picture. He neglects not one detail. In order to walk with Him and trust Him, we need His perspective. We are carriers of His vision. How small-minded of us to think our desires for fullness and fruitfulness came from us. It is by design. We were created to be fruitful—to go forth and multiply (see Genesis 1:28).

This can refer to multiplying generations, of course. But that is not all we are called to multiply! We are also called to multiply goodness. What is the good fruit you want to multiply in your life? God wants you to write down the vision and make it plain (Habakkuk 2:2). He wants to reveal truth to you about what is up ahead in your journey. But how well you know His heart will determine your perspective. We cannot be a people who quit at the first sign of trouble. We need to learn from Joshua and Caleb.

Nevertheless

Remember how Naomi stopped urging Ruth after she recognized Ruth's determination? Jesus left speaking with Simon Peter for another reason. Jesus stopped speaking His lesson on the boat to demonstrate His lesson. Jesus wanted to teach, not just with words but with actions. Jesus gave Peter this direction in Luke 5: "When He had stopped speaking, He said to Simon, 'Launch out into the deep and let down your nets for a catch.' But Simon answered and said to Him, 'Master, we have toiled all night and caught nothing; nevertheless at Your word I will let down the net'" (Luke 5:4–5 NKJV).

There's a principle here in these verses that we need to grasp. No matter what it looks like; no matter what human reasoning tells us; no matter what we've done before to no avail; at your word, Lord, we will let down the net. At your word, we obey. At your word, we cast all other reasoning aside. This was Peter's "nevertheless" experience. This was the moment he decided to obey regardless of the odds. He set his mind on what the Lord had commanded. We often forget that "God said" is a command. A command is not optional if we want to live an exceptional life. Doing what God says to do is a necessity in order to fully walk in what God has for us.

Peter obeyed because the Lord told him to do something. It was a command. Peter was not doing it because he thought it was sensible. He cast his net because he knew the One with him was able to do something greater.

And just what did Peter experience when he let down his net? "And when they had done this, they caught a great number of fish, and their net was breaking. So they signaled to their partners in the other boat to come and help them. And they came and filled both the boats, so that they began to sink" (Luke 5:6–7 NKJV).

Peter caught so many fish that his boat *and* another boat began to sink under the weight of the great thing God did! It was so much greater than he ever could have imagined! Does this sound familiar? God wants to give us a life that is beyond what we know through our human reasoning. It requires of us a "nevertheless" mindset. We must have a fixed determination to say, "Yes— nevertheless. At your word, I let down my net. At your word, I follow, even when it doesn't make sense." Peter's "nevertheless" experience was met in a remarkable way. I believe your "nevertheless" experience will be met in a remarkable way, too! It will pay dividends over and over! You will reap so much blessing that it will overflow to those around you. I know this because of my own "nevertheless" experience.

Yes, Lord

My "nevertheless" experience began with a question from God. It was an October Friday night, and there was a special church service. I almost didn't go, but praise God I did. Not knowing it yet, I walked into a defining moment of my life. I went down to the altar to pray for healing. I was believing for something instantaneous, but the Lord had something greater in mind, because a prayer answered in an instant has the potential to leave a pattern of seeking answers, not seeking the Lord.

That October night in 2012, I embarked on the journey that has changed my life and my faith. The woman praying for me had asked before agreeing with me, "What do you want?" And I said, "I want to walk without my crutches." As I was being prayed for, I didn't physically feel any different. I simply heard the Lord ask one thing. And, in my spirit, I knew what that involved. The Lord so impressed upon my heart this important question: "Do you trust Me?"

"Yes, Lord, I trust You," I replied. I have replied with trust every day since as I walk hand-in-hand with my Jesus one step at a time. Walking without crutches is not always easy, but it's worth it. I trust God to take my impossibilities and turn them into possibilities. I don't have anything to go on but the Lord's Word. That's the only thing we need—if we're brave enough to say, "Nevertheless."

The Secret of Joshua and Caleb

I believe Joshua and Caleb had a "nevertheless" mindset. They had a higher perspective than the average Israelite. I believe God has shown me the secret in scripture that reveals the source of this greater perspective. Why were they filled with faith during the assignment they were given? Why were they enabled out of all the spies to see possibility? Why were they different?

The assignment was given in Numbers 13:2: "Send out men to explore the land of Canaan, the land I am giving to the Israelites. Send one leader from each of the twelve ancestral tribes." Twelve men were chosen to spy out the land. The specific command goes on to say: "See what the land is like, and find out whether the people living there are strong or weak, few or many. See what kind of land they live in. Is it good or bad? Do their towns have walls, or are they unprotected like open camps? Is the soil fertile or poor? Are there many trees? Do your best to bring back samples of the crops you see. (It happened to be the season for harvesting the first ripe grapes.)" (Numbers 13:18–20 NLT). These twelve men were sent as the leaders of their tribes to explore the land God wanted to give them and to report back their findings. Their findings turned out to be 2 versus 10: two for and ten against taking the land.

The Israelites all had the same promise. God's presence was promised to be with them wherever they went and bring them into a promised land. Yet the reports varied about the same land. Two saw a land of promise, and ten saw a land too great for them. The two who saw through the eyes of possibility were Joshua and Caleb. Here's what sets them apart: out of the spies, Joshua spent the most time with Moses. Moses was God's chosen representative to deliver the Israelites from captivity to the promise. God spoke with Moses and gave him direction to deliver this group of people. Joshua talked to Moses and learned first-hand from this leader. I found a powerful secret in (Exodus 33:11 NLT): "Inside the Tent of Meeting, the Lord would speak to Moses face to face, as one speaks to a friend. Afterward Moses would return to the camp, but the young man who assisted him, Joshua son of Nun, would remain behind in the Tent of Meeting." God speaking to Moses as with a friend is a powerful truth, but the fact that Joshua stayed in the tent is the secret.

Joshua could see far beyond the other Israelites because of his association with Moses. Joshua was assigned to help Moses, and because of this, he got a closer look at the things of God. But, I believe Joshua went beyond his duties when he decided to stay in the Tent of Meeting. The Tent of Meeting represents the Tabernacle, the Sanctuary of God, the dwelling place of His presence. In the Tent of Meeting, God spoke. In the Tent of Meeting, strategy was given for the promise. In the Tent of Meeting, God shared how He would meet needs. Joshua lingered in the Tent of Meeting. In today's terms, Joshua remained in the Secret Place. Joshua was not a stranger to God's private presence. Joshua made a point to stay where he would meet with God. I have to think that because of Moses' influence on Joshua's life, he learned the importance of dwelling in God's presence. Joshua was distinguished, set apart, and developed as the successor to Moses because of His time abiding in the presence of God.

Just as Joshua's time in the Secret Place distinguished him, our time in the Secret Place will distinguish us, too. It will separate us and give us God's presence, His power, and His mandate. Joshua's access to the Tent of Meeting was no accident. It was by design. God knew he would need to be influenced by time with Moses to take the promised land. Moses was the one who knew the Promise Giver the most intimately. But, as we see in the Bible, Joshua was not the only spy with a good report. Joshua and Caleb both believed the good report. I believe Caleb was influenced greatly by Joshua. Perhaps they stuck together and spent the most time together out of any of the other twelve. Caleb knew what God had promised, and he believed God for it. But, as he spent more and more time with Joshua, he must have heard many stories about God encounters in the Tent of Meeting. As a result, Caleb's heart trusted in God. He wanted to be a part of what God was doing.

If you want to be a part of what God is doing, take heart, and follow Caleb's example. Walk knowing who your God is and what He wants to do. The other ten spies reported impossibility to inherit the land. They explored and reported on the land and the people in it, just as they were told to do. They noticed that the people were bigger, stronger, and more able. What they failed to realize was the power of the presence with them. Only

Joshua and Caleb knew and understood the significance of the presence. They knew God was good to keep His promise—nevertheless—even though it seemed impossible. Nevertheless, God was—and is—able. All twelve spies saw the same fruit, the same land flowing with milk and honey. But Caleb was the one that said, "We should go up and take possession of the land, for we can certainly do it" (Numbers 13:30 NIV).

Caleb was able to give this good report because of his ability to see through the lens of promise. He saw possibility where others saw strong adversaries. Joshua and Caleb knew God was stronger than anyone or anything they could ever face. The people of Israel believed the report of the ten—the majority—and wanted to turn back to Egyptian captivity. But believing the majority isn't always the best thing. The safest and boldest thing to do is to follow God. God was pleased with Caleb and how determined he was to walk in the promise. "But because my servant Caleb has a different spirit and follows me wholeheartedly, I will bring him into the land he went to, and his descendants will inherit it" (Numbers 14:24 NIV). Caleb's determination to partner with God guaranteed that he would see the promised land—he and his generations to come!

The Different Spirit

Caleb's different spirit caught the eye of God. His spirit and his wholehearted trust in God brought him a great inheritance. His spirit was strong and able to withstand the promise. He was able to stay in God's presence and not waver from what God had declared. His spirit was steadfast.

David said, "Create in me a pure heart, O God, and renew a steadfast spirit within me. Do not cast me from your presence or take your Holy Spirit from me. Restore to me the joy of your salvation and grant me a willing spirit, to sustain me" (Psalm 51:10–12 NIV).

A steadfast spirit is required for this journey, and it has to be renewed, as David shows us. It's not going to be maintained by only one choice; it's a continual choice. There are times that your spirit will be tested. But, after the test, if you press on, you are made even stronger. This is a continual walk I am on, and I am determined to not relent. I want to press on to see the fullness of God in my life. But, as we take ground, the enemy will come to steal it. That's why we have to keep renewing our spirits. Pray Psalm 51 in your own words: "God! Create in me a heart of purity and a steadfast spirit. Don't take your presence from me. I don't want to go if you're not there. Sustain me."

I promise you, friends, God is right here with us. If you have the heart to follow after Him, He will sustain you. God not only provided manna in the wilderness but streams, too. He provides for us spiritually as well as physically. Renew your spirit and renew your strength with His divine source of provision.

Opt Out

Sitting in disbelief of hard circumstances, you may feel like asking, "Can I just opt out? Can I go the easy route?

Can I not experience this pain?" One day, I remember thinking, "Lord, I just want to opt out of this one. I've been through this test before. I passed. I'll pass. Let's skip this. God, you can make it like it never happened." I was rear-ended just days before and reinjured my neck on top of much degeneration. One day, before getting e-stimulation treatment, I asked my doctor, "Can I just opt out?"

Without hesitation, he said, "No."

That word was not spoken to be restrictive, but to be good for me. No, you need this. Just because you want to avoid pain does not mean that it will disappear. Opting out of the process of healing will not change the past. It will only keep you from the outcome. And, more importantly, you can't opt out and maintain a steadfast spirit. Temptation to abdicate will come, but press in and see the faithfulness of God. He is working all things for your good. I'm telling you, you cannot quit. These words are not meant to limit you, but to enlarge you. Nothing good comes from quitting when things get hard. It just leaves you stuck. If we stay in the wilderness, we will not see the promise. The wilderness is not the destination. It is the pathway to trust. Our job is not to figure out "why" we're in this situation, but to believe God at all times.

Always, Never

There's no expiration date on what the Lord wants to do. Don't let your "hope deferred" become "praise deferred."

Hope deferred makes the heart sick,
but a longing fulfilled is a tree of life."
(Proverbs 13:12 NIV)

Hold fast to the promise of God in your life; never let go. Do you know what you are doing when you "give up"? You're giving up the chance for new territory—to behold the promise. I'll cover more of that throughout the book.

God knows this season is hard. He knows you are being tempted to give up. That's why He is singing a lullaby over you in the storm. He's saying to you, "Don't give up." And He is singing His own personal lullaby over you to bring you peace and rest. Listen to the song.

Promises do not have expiration dates, but it's tempting to set deadlines. Deadlines are useful for completing goals, but they can also steal your hope. The God of the universe, the God who created the moon and the stars, and you, is the One who gave you the promise. You know it deep within your bones, down to the tips of your toes. It is engrafted in your spirit. You are ready to see the promise fulfilled, so you think you'll see it happen this year or maybe next. Hope connected to a timeframe is great, but if the promise doesn't come in your timeframe, I beg you, do not cast aside your faith and hope. What God says is sure. Abraham had to wait twenty-five years, but God's promise to him was fulfilled and continued. The impatience and "give up" spirit in today's culture is destroying our trust in God.

Humans are so quick to get discouraged. Ironically, though, when we order something online, we do not immediately go to the mailbox or doorstep. We know it has a proper estimated time of arrival, or ETA. God's promise has an ETA, too. Just because the package or the promise isn't here today, doesn't mean it's not coming. Wait for it!

I want to show you what God has taught me about being steadfast. In Luke 18, Jesus taught about the persistent widow. "One day Jesus told his disciples a story to show that they should always pray and never give up" (Luke 18:1 NLT).

In school, I remember being taught to not use absolutes in writing. Teachers said to refrain from using words like "always" and "never." But this is God's absolute truth: we should *always* pray, and we should *never* give up. Always pray and never give up applies to any situation as long as we put it in God's hands!

There is a *defining moment* that we all come to in our lives. Are we going to give up and forfeit the promise, or are we going to press on and take hold of it? The choice is yours. But, if you have a word from God, I want to encourage you to stand strong! That is all you need! Search the Word for promises to stand on, and write down what He spoke to your heart personally. He is faithful even to His personal promises to us, down to the last detail! David's son speaks of God's detailed faithfulness:

> Before the entire congregation of Israel,
> Solomon took a position before the Altar,
> spread his hands out before heaven, and

prayed, O God, God of Israel, there is no God like you in the skies above or on the earth below who unswervingly keeps covenant with his servants and relentlessly loves them as they sincerely live in obedience to your way. You kept your word to David my father, your personal word. You did exactly what you promised—every detail. The proof is before us today! Keep it up, God, O God of Israel! Continue to keep the promises you made to David my father when you said, "You'll always have a descendant to represent my rule on Israel's throne, on the condition that your sons are as careful to live obediently in my presence as you have. O God of Israel, let this all happen; confirm and establish it!" (1 Kings 8:22–26 MSG)

Prayer is beautiful communication with God. I love prayer! Praise God we have the ability to come boldly into the Throne Room. My favorite thing to do in prayer is to give thanks to God and just talk to Him.

I work for a ministry, and I love that my coworkers come to me with their prayer requests! It is such an honor to pray for others. Sometimes, I sense that people think I know a secret to powerful prayers. It's not a secret, and it's really simple, actually. I believe the power of God responds because I know I have access to Him. I don't have to pray with a religious formula; I can reverence Him and talk to Him as a friend. I know beyond a shadow of a doubt that He hears me. We don't have to beg God to move for us, but we do have to persevere.

I have experienced a quiet confidence, knowing that my God hears me even if I whisper. I don't have to repeat myself or shout (although I can). There's nothing wrong with that. I just know that God is close. He shows me that He's near, and it gives me unexplainable joy. No matter the pain we face from day to day, nothing compares to knowing Him and believing Him. Waiting on Him was never promised to be easy, but thank God for communion with Him and His Holy Spirit. I have found that I am closer to God because of my adversity, and I have developed a stronger trust in Him. There's a level of provision and constant awareness of His presence that I would not have known if I were not dependent on Him. Because I am weak, He is strong for me (see 2 Corinthians 12:9).

"This is the confidence we have in approaching God: that if we ask anything according to his will, he hears us. And if we know that he hears us—whatever we ask— we know that we have what we asked of him" (1 John 5:14–15 NIV).

Our confidence lies in Jesus and knowing that the Father hears us. And, not only that He hears us, but that when we pray according to His will, we *have* what we ask of Him. You can't receive more confidence than that! Our God is so faithful, and I pray that as you read this book you'll discover that to an outstanding degree.

In the Old Testament, sacrifice was the standard to get God's attention. But now our obedience is the key. We know our prayers rise and get His attention (see Revelation 8:3–4). The angels are given charge to make sure the prayers of the saints are tended to by the Lord. If you have the slightest doubt that God hears you, remember the angels, too. Expect miracles. God is not too busy for you. He is the Alpha and the Omega. The Beginning and the End. The Great Physician. He is Sovereign, and He knows the exact time to sweep in to your situation. He is the El Shaddai—God Almighty, the Great I *Am*. He *is* working for you right now!

God is not slow in keeping His promises to you. He is ready to walk you into His promise. Do you trust Him? Steadfast one, let's get ready for what is up ahead.

Cluster

Joshua and Caleb—the ones who believed God and walked right into the fullness—didn't listen to fear. It's not that they were super human; it's just that they had a strong spirit that believed God. They didn't listen to the negative reports. They gave higher reports and had substance to show for it. They obeyed fully in what they were asked to do, and they brought back fruit from the land to show that it was "exceedingly good."

"Then they came to the Valley of Eshcol, and there cut down a branch with one cluster of grapes; they carried between two of them on a pole. They also brought some of the pomegranates and figs. The place was called the

Valley of Eshcol, because of the cluster which the men of Israel cut down there. And they returned from spying out the land after forty days. Now they departed and came back to Moses and Aaron and all the congregation of the children of Israel in the Wilderness of Paran, at Kadesh; they brought back word to them and to all the congregation, and showed them the fruit of the land. Then they told him, and said: "We went to the land where you sent us. It truly flows with milk and honey, and this is its fruit" (Numbers 13:23–27 NIV).

I love how Joshua and Caleb named the valley where the fruit came from! I love that they were bold enough to carry fruit back with them even though they did not possess the land yet. I want you to imagine this cluster of fruit. I want you to see that your promised land truly flows with God's goodness, His milk and honey. I want you to imagine the fruit of God's promise to you in advance. Picture it; write it down. Every detail that you can think of. Your steadfast spirit needs this substance to cling to before you see the physical evidence. When you write this down, your promise is surrounded by faith.

I believe you're going to be able to name your valley of God's promise because you could see the fruit, the goodness, and the promise. I believe you're going to name that season, because you're not staying there. You are not giving up! You are moving on to take possession of all that God said you can have!

— **TWO** —

Stability Training

Therefore put on the full armor of God, so that when the day of evil comes, you may be able to stand your ground, and after you have done everything, to stand.

—Ephesians 6:13 (NIV)

Walking on Sand

> So don't sit around on your hands! No more dragging your feet! Clear the path for long-distance runners so no one will trip and fall, so no one will step in a hole and sprain an ankle. Help each other out. And run for it. (Hebrews 12:12–13, MSG)

As I read Hebrews 12:13 on the way to a beach vacation, it jumped up off the page as if God were talking just to me. I told the Lord, "I'm doing all I can. I can't seem to make a straight path for my feet."

But little did know that God wasn't telling me to try harder. He was telling me ahead of time how hard He was working for me! When I got to the beach, it was just days after a tropical storm. This storm cleared a straight path for me. The sand was packed tight, and I was able to walk unassisted on the beach for the first time in my life! As a teenager, I attended beach camp with my youth group. I used to dream about being able to walk along the beach with my friends. That day on vacation, I finally got to see my dream come true.

The Trainer

On average days, our promise seems so far away. The goal can seem unattainable. Impossibility can overwhelm us. Each time I fall, I'm reminded how big my impossibility—walking—seems. I have learned on this journey that God is like my personal trainer. I have to listen for the words of my trainer to help me get back up. Without those words, I am lost in the realm of impossibility. But, with the trainer's invaluable instruction, I am miraculously brought into the realm of possibility. My trainer—God—helps me up every time I fall. He always sends His helping hand. He always makes sure I have what I need.

The fall of man came about by listening to the wrong words. Man listened to twisted lies above God's instructions. And, like Adam and Eve, we all at some point fall to fear and shame. But, God wants us to be standing. The enemy will knock us down, but because of God's training, we can get back up.

There's a movie I've seen in which a woman gets trained in self-defense. Her trainer tells her that her attacker will knock her down, and he will think he has won. The trainer tells her that when (not if) this occurs, it is the most crucial moment. And just like the attacker, the enemy thinks he is in a prime position to take you out when you're down.

Imagine you are on the ground and your strength is gone. Your enemy is behind you. But, when you lift up your eyes, you see your Savior's hand extended, ready to help you up. As you gaze on Him, you remember your training. You remember His words, His truth.

You are more than a conqueror (Romans 8:37), and you can do *all* things through Christ who strengthens you (Philippians 4:13). You are infused with strength as you take His hand. You rise and Jesus causes your enemy to scatter, and ultimately scripture says God makes our enemies our footstool (Hebrews 1:13 and Luke 20:43). A footstool is to rest under your feet. God shows us in our training that the enemy is under our feet!

When we stand, we have the advantage! When we lose our place and fall, the enemy, your attacker, thinks he has won. But, when God trains you and raises you up, He speaks truth. The enemy wants to lie to you and instill fear, shame, and condemnation. God equips us for everything we face.

God's truth adjusts your armor, and He hands you His shield of faith. Now, instead of taking so much time to gain your footing, God's truth restores you as you had never fallen. The enemy will try to attack back, but listen to Jesus, look to Him, resist the devil (James 4:7), and stand your ground.

Stability Training

Sand is unstable. It moves and shifts. That day on the beach, God was able to take something unstable and make it stable in my life. He is our solid rock.

> Therefore everyone who hears these words of mine and puts them into practice is like a wise man who built his house on the rock. The rain came down, the streams rose, and the winds blew and beat against that house; yet it did not fall, because it had its foundation on the rock. But everyone who hears these words of mine and does not put them into practice is like a foolish man who built his house on sand. (Matthew 7:24–26 NIV)

To be stable, we must build our lives on God's Word. We must act upon His Words. We have to believe Him before our circumstances make sense.

The Armor of God gives us the advantage over the enemy. It enables us to remain standing during the fight. We stand in the power of God's might (see Ephesians 6:10).

Lately, I've encountered a lot of people with needs in their physical health. Prolonged illness, disability, or pain wears a person down. Exhaustion and disappointment can settle in. But do not be deceived!

A physical need does not mean it's a different fight. We still do not wrestle against flesh and blood. Pain and trouble in your body is not God's plan. It's the plan of the enemy. Satan comes against people to stop them from walking into their destiny. But do you know what? God is big enough to work all things together for our good (see Romans 8:28).

Our lack of strength does not disqualify us. We are strong and made stable in God's might. On my own my balance is weak, but with God by my side, I am strong. He is the One who hands me His armor when I fall.

His armor is this: the belt of truth, the breastplate of righteousness, the preparation of the gospel of peace, the shield of faith (above all), the helmet of salvation, and the sword of the Spirit which is the Word of God (see Ephesians 6:10–20).

The same armor is recommended for every fight. We must utilize what God has given to us. He has given us His armor. His strength. We must learn from Him. We must receive His love *and* His discipline. It's His training for battle.

His Training

Every fighting champion has a cornerman. It's the person wiping the blood and sweat away—the person staring the fighter in the face, speaking confidence into his or her soul.

God is my trainer and my Champion. I have put all my confidence in the One who speaks to me. Without God—the Champion of champions—in my corner, I am nothing. Without Him, I would be down for the count.

Oh, but with Him! With God is my corner, there is nothing I cannot do! He is not only Trainer but my Creator! He knows how to pull out the best in me because He placed it there!

He Can Train You, Too.

You can allow God to become your trainer by creating an environment in your life that makes room for Him to speak.

The word "ability" can be found within the word "stability." According to dictionary.com, *stability* means "being stable; one's firmness in position; or steadfastness, constancy as in character and purpose."[4] Steadfastness is a characteristic that is important in all areas of life. It is important for us to establish true stability in Christ because our ability cannot come from our own strength. It comes from God. So, we must let Him teach us about true stability.

The storms of life will not be able to shake God's solid foundation. Do you want to remain steadfast in life? You have to start with your foundation.

> Wisdom is the principal thing; Therefore get wisdom. And in all your getting, get understanding. Exalt her, and she will

promote you; She will bring you honor, when you embrace her. She will place on your head an ornament of grace; A crown of glory she will deliver to you. (Proverbs 4:7–9 NKJV)

Wisdom is the foundation we build on—God's instruction. What is God's instruction for you? What does the Bible say? What is His personal word?

Might I suggest that God has already tried to train you? He has been speaking; we just need ears to hear. We know we hear when we are in His Word. Wisdom will deliver you to His promises. Listen to His voice.

God trains us with His armor, His Word, His voice, and His presence. He guards us, and He reinforces us with weapons of His realm—His Word, His voice, and His say in our lives—and He will never leave us or forsake us! He is with us always!

Track Record

A track record shows the history of wins and losses. It commemorates the score of past successes and achievements of an individual or team. I like to think of my history with God as just that—a track record of wins. Remember Ruth, the first person recorded as steadfast in the Bible? She did not have a track record, or history with God, to look back on. Abraham did not have a track record with God, either. Yet they both eventually had many victories and successes to record.

Just like Ruth and Abraham, we must believe in God and His promises before we can even see them.

Our faith is pleasing to God, and He responds on our behalf!

> But without faith it is impossible to [walk with God and] please Him, for whoever comes [near] to God must [necessarily] believe that God exists and that He rewards those who [earnestly and diligently] seek Him. (Hebrews 11:6 AMP)

The Power of Reps

I am not proud of this habit, but I've got to be honest. When someone tells me to do more repetitions (reps) of an exercise, I've been known to cut my eyes at the person and smile sarcastically. It's like my brain has communicated a message of "Really? Great!—*not!*" to my face. I'm trying to improve this. (My apologies, especially to my doctor. You've seen that look too many times. Thanks for always calling me out on it, and making me laugh!)

There is power in repetition. It's the power of "re." "Re" is a prefix that means "to do again." To repeat, if you will. "Re" will give you the advantage of consistency. What you consistently do, you reap the benefits of. If you are consistently going to work, you will get a paycheck. If you consistently renew your mind, you will think on truth. If you consistently tithe, God will bless and provide for you. If you consistently seek Him, God will guide you. I hear my trainer consistently say:

- Again.
- Keep your eyes on Me.
- Don't stop.
- Don't give up.
- It's not over.

As we learn to hear the voice of God, He trains us how to carry out His will. But there are things that will try to come against us. The biggest obstacle that will come against you is not your circumstance or situation; it will be the fear you face.

- The fear of failure
- The fear of giants
- The fear of not being strong enough to handle the journey

The training voice of God is always building up. It always edifies. It always encourages. Our Trainer does not condemn. He calls out the best in us. If you are discouraged by your trainer, I think it's safe to say we don't have the same one! God is always pushing me because there is something greater ahead. He is not overbearing. Quite the opposite! He carries my burdens for me. His training reminds me to let Him do the heavy lifting.

When I feel overwhelmed, it is because I have entertained the wrong voice—fear.

> For God has not given us a spirit of fear
> and timidity, but of power, love, and self-
> discipline. (2 Timothy 1:7 NLT)

Do not fear! God gives us the power, love, and self-discipline needed to fulfill His call. As we obey God's guidance and His training, we are more and more equipped for this steadfast journey.

Sometimes we may not understand why things happen as they do, or why God is calling us to take certain steps. That's okay. What's important is to understand is that our Trainer knows best!

Trainer Knows Best

These steps and repetitions are training for what is ahead of us. If I had chosen to go by my own understanding, thoughts, and feelings, I would have considered myself disqualified by now. But God is not interested in how qualified you think you are. He's interested in you letting Him qualify you for what He's called you to.

On my own, my weaknesses far outweigh my strength. I bought a stability ball years ago because I wanted to exercise more regularly. Balance is a huge struggle for me. It is one of the things that makes walking so difficult. When I bought this ball, I thought I would use it to practice building my core strength and balance. But I ended up getting on that ball and wobbling until I collapsed in a fit of laughter.

I disqualified myself from reaping the benefits of

using the stability ball. *I'm just not stable enough*, I thought. The enemy loves to be in the business of disqualifying us. All he has to do is make us believe a lie.

- I can't.
- I'm unfit.
- I'm disqualified.
- I'm unable.
- I'm too this or that.

The list goes on and on! It's only when we have His power and truth to overcome those lies that we will try again.

I tried using my stability ball again today. There was no crashing in a fit of laughter this time. I actually got to use the stability ball the way it was intended. I say this to encourage you that just because you've never seen success in a certain area, don't let that keep you from trying! Don't let anything limit you. You can do this! You can try again!

I recently heard a man of God teach on finances. He said, "If you don't tell your money where to go, you'll ask where it's been." The same principle is true in many areas. If we don't tell our future where to go, we'll just focus on where we've been.

I don't want to stay where I am, and I don't think you do either. We want to walk into even greater things. In order to do so, we must focus on our training. Our Trainer is strengthening us and equipping us to bring us into greater things.

Weight Training

Weight training is necessary to build strength, endurance, and steadfastness. In God's type of training, you gain experience in both weight training and *wait* training. Waiting is a part of weight training because it is the main key to developing endurance to see lasting results. Weights give muscles resistance to push back on. In physical fitness, I know I need to lift weights more. I need to build my tolerance for resistance. I need to push past barriers to see growth, improvement, and change in my body. The same is true for our spiritual muscles.

It's necessary to push past limits to reach our potential. Is there an area where you have plateaued in your routine? Me, too. That's why it's imperative that I remain consistent in my training. I keep walking because I don't want to lose ground that is mine for the taking. Walking is my daily reminder that there are more miracles ahead.

What is it you need training for? You have to keep a vision in front of you. Your God-given vision will motivate you to keep going. Keep training! You're going to walk into what you are believing for if you don't quit!

Starting Point

All through my life, I have always wanted better balance. One day, I asked my doctor for exercise advance. He gave me exercises to do, and I did them, but not for long. My doctor told me it was going to take at least two years (no exaggeration) for me to see a change in my balance. I didn't want to wait that long. I got discouraged because it didn't seem to work after a few weeks. But, more than my lack of patience, I think I had a lack of vision.

I couldn't see the finish from the starting point. Now, looking back, I wish I had stuck with it. Even though we can't see the finish line at the beginning, somewhere along the way, we will see progress. That's what trainers (both God and other wise experts) have the ability to see. They have trained eyes to notice progress and potential.

If I had stuck with my exercises, I would've been in the company of progress. However, since I decided to not work towards better balance with exercise, I forfeited the reward and an opportunity for training.

Training is a discipline you cannot move forward without. We all need it!

Agonizing over your weakness does not change anything. Get up, do what you can, and be consistent. I'm telling you, it's worth it! We don't have to be able or strong to be trained by God. The first thing we need to do is realize we need His help. We're nothing without Him!

Here are a few ways to listen to your trainer:

- Trust the leadership of God and those God ordains in your life.
- If you resist guidance, it's unlikely you will go very far. (You'll probably just go in circles!)
- Make a new commitment to listen to wisdom.
- Read the trainer's manual. (Yes, of course, it's the Bible.)

Those are your first steps. You will grow strong as you keep training by:

- Staying in scripture—if you're not sure where to start, try reading the Psalms, the book of John, Ephesians 6, or another passage of your choice.
- Making a habit of prayer.
- Asking God to speak to you. What is your Trainer telling you to do?
- Writing His instructions. Keep it before your eyes.

> Write the vision
> And make it plain on tablets,
> That he may run who reads it.
> For the vision is yet for an appointed time;
> But at the end it will speak, and it will not lie.
> Though it tarries, wait for it;
> Because it will surely come,
> It will not tarry. (Habakkuk 2:2–3 NKJV)

Many things can distract you from your vision. Write down His promise to remind yourself of His truth. Keep your focus. Stay in your training. The more you keep the vision in front of you, the more likely you are to fulfill it, because you know where you want or need to go.

I have been privileged to be surrounded by people who encourage me in my faith. With their input and safeguard of wise counsel, I am reminded of my training. But I love it when I encounter wise people who not only remind me of solid ways to train and grow but remind me of my Trainer. It's people who remind you of God that will leave you inspired.

God is so very patient with us. I've encountered His persistent patience with me over and over. Recently, I had an injury that set me back in my goals. I didn't want anything to take away my progress of walking, so I kept at it. But I was even slower than my normal pace. I wanted to move around as normal, but my body physically would not let me. Every time I could not do something on my own, God patiently waited on me. He didn't rush me to do or to perform. He showed His patience and His kindness to me through His people.

I remember one morning in particular being so frustrated with myself. I wanted to walk from my car to the door, and I must have tried ten to twenty times to steady myself. I thought if I could just get my balance, I could will myself to move. I had a reality check—that's not how cerebral palsy works. I understand that I can't will myself to "just do it." But, at the same time, my faith believes in the impossible. I've seen it, and I step into it every day—literally!—with every movement.

But that morning, and many others, I encounter grace and patience and assistance in the form of a helping hand. God sends someone at just the right time, and athough I'm frustrated with myself, God never is. He is so patient and loving. So kind and tender. He never pushes me, but sometimes His hand is the only one there with me. He is my strong side. He is my constant. He not only trains me; He steadies me.

Who Steadies You?

Just as God is with me every step, He wants you to know He is with you. You may not be aware of His presence, but He is definitely there. He is constant and steady in your life, too. How have you seen Him show up? Do you notice Him in your day-to-day life?

Purpose

Our Trainer, God, does not train us just to train us. It's not just because He can. He trains us for a purpose! He thinks about equipping us for the future. He has given us His armor; do you know what do with it? How do you wear it? How do you wield your sword—the Word of God? How do you stand on your feet as a great army (Ezekiel 37:10)? We not only hear the Word of God—we speak it! We say what God is saying! Listening is good; hearing the instruction of our commander is good; obeying orders is better. Soldiers in the Lord's army should take orders as they are commanded. With the sword of the Spirit, we have a living and active Word. It is effective in battle. But it doesn't move because of what we have heard; it moves because we utilize it. We speak it! We proclaim and prophesy the Word of God with our own voice.

Have you used your sword lately? It is ready for battle? We have more access to the Word of God than any generation before us. We can download an app on any device. It's time for God's army to stand. You've received training from God, and now there are victories to win in His name!

We are not defenseless. We are not weak. We are equipped! When God sees us, He sees warriors! We are called according to His purpose (see Romans 8:28). Shouldn't we take our place? Let's advance!

— THREE —

Hold Fast

Let us hold unswervingly to the hope we profess, for He who promised is faithful.

—Hebrews 10:23 (NIV)

Speaking to Valleys and Mountains

The way you hold fast to something is by taking a firm grip on it. To set the stage for this chapter, we will cover a lot of scripture. My prayer is that each passage stirs your heart to strengthen your grip on hope.

In Ezekiel 37, we read about the valley of dry bones. The Lord set Ezekiel in a valley and let him pass by all of the dry bones. The first thing we see God speak to Ezekiel is a question, and the second is a command in Ezekiel 37:1–10 (NKJV):

> The hand of the LORD came upon me
> and brought me out in the Spirit of the
> LORD, and set me down in the midst of

the valley; and it was full of bones. Then He caused me to pass by them all around, and behold, there were very many in the open valley; and indeed they were very dry. And He said to me, "Son of man, can these bones live?" So I answered, "O Lord GOD, You know."

This is the question God asked, "Can these bones live?" Life had gone from them, but God wanted to know whether this man believed that life could come again. If you believe, then you will do whatever God tells you to do.

Again He said to me, "Prophesy to these bones, and say to them, 'O dry bones, hear the word of the LORD! Thus says the Lord GOD to these bones: "Surely I will cause breath to enter into you, and you shall live. I will put sinews on you and bring flesh upon you, cover you with skin and put breath in you; and you shall live. Then you shall know that I am the LORD." ' "So I prophesied as I was commanded; and as I prophesied, there was a noise, and suddenly a rattling; and the bones came together, bone to bone. Indeed, as I looked, the sinews and the flesh came upon them, and the skin covered them over; but there was

> no breath in them. Also He said to me,
> "Prophesy to the breath, prophesy, son of
> man, and say to the breath, 'Thus says the
> Lord God: "Come from the four winds,
> O breath, and breathe on these slain, that
> they may live." ' " So I prophesied as He
> commanded me, and breath came into
> them, and they lived, and stood upon
> their feet, an exceedingly great army."

When we prophesy as God commands us, when we speak what He speaks, then what looks impossible will become possible for us. There will a great army standing on their feet. This is proof that when God speaks, and when we agree with Him, there is great life-giving power available!

Even the disciples were amazed at the power in the words Jesus spoke. In Mark 11, the disciples saw a fig tree dry at the roots because Jesus, seeing it was unfruitful, commanded it to never be fruitful again. Peter cried out, "Rabbi, look!" Pointing to the tree, I imagine he was filled with wonder. *Look, everything obeys Him.* It's similar to the amazement we still experience today with prophecy. *Look! Didn't you declare this before it happened?*

> So Jesus answered and said to them,
> "Have faith in God. For assuredly, I say
> to you, whoever says to this mountain,
> 'Be removed and be cast into the sea,' and
> does not doubt in his heart, but believes

that those things he says will be done, he will have whatever he says. Therefore I say to you, whatever things you ask when you pray, believe that you receive them, and you will have them." (Mark 11:22–24 NKJV)

Jesus reveals to us that if we speak in faith, things happen. He commanded a tree to whither, but He didn't use the tree as an example when He taught His disciples the power of our faith filled words (in Mark 11). He used a greater example. He referenced a mountain!

Our faith can flow through our words, and our words can raise up every valley and move every mountain. Our words are powerful! Are you beginning to see how important it is to raise your voice? I hope you will make a commitment to speak in agreement with what God says. Because when we say what God prompts us to say, our faith will be unstoppable. There's no limit to what God will do!

Meditating on the Word

So then, how do we speak what God says?

To speak what He says, we have to know what He says! We have to read His Word and delight in it. As a teenager, I made lists of scriptures on certain topics so that could pray the Word over situations. I put the lists in a binder that I called my scripture notebook. I almost forgot about the notebook—but I'll never forget the words written inside. Those scriptures were not just words on printed pages; they were and are imprinted on my heart.

We as Christians should strive to be so full of the Word of God that we don't think about scripture only when we're reading it on a screen or on paper. We should be so full of the Word that is in our heart at all times. God said in Joshua 1:8 (NLT), "Study this Book of Instruction continually. Meditate on it day and night so you will be sure to obey everything written in it. Only then will you prosper and succeed in all you do." He really meant for us to meditate on it day *and* night. We are to fix our minds on His instruction so much so that we think on it not just in our waking hours but also in our sleep.

The Message version of the Bible starts off Psalm 91 like this: "You who sit down in the High God's presence, spend the night in Shaddai's shadow." We can even sleep under the shadow of the Almighty! That's an example of what I would call meditating on God day and night—when we dwell with Him always.

I don't know about you, but I want victory even in my sleep. I want to meditate day and night, but that is determined by my input. You may have heard this phrase before: *We are products of our input.* What do you allow in your mind? What you are seeing and hearing the most has a big impact on what you think on. That's why meditating on the Word requires us to increase our intake of the Word of God.

To increase our dedication to the Word, we have to be intentional! Growth does not come easily. Some may choose to get up earlier and read the Bible, while some may choose to listen to the Bible on audio or sermons during a commute to work. Some may choose to reduce distractions such as time spent watching television and social media daily. Some may even feel that it is best to implement all of the above for a season. We all have to find ways to make room for Him.

> Blessed are those who hunger and thirst
> for righteousness, for they will be filled.
> (Matthew 5:6 NIV)

What are you going to choose to be hungry for?

Standing Firm in Your Goals

Your input—through your eyes, ears, and ultimately your thoughts—also affects your goals. Do you have staying power to complete your goals? The majority of people in America—more than 80 percent—don't reach their own New Year's resolutions. According to the American Psychological Association: "Research has found that even when people's willpower is wavering, they will persist with tasks requiring self-control if they're told they will be rewarded or that their efforts will benefit others."[5] You are more likely to be persistent and unwavering if you recognize the ways your efforts will benefit yourself and, most importantly, others. There are promises for those who commit to hold fast. In other words, there is a benefit—our hard work pays off—if we persist.

If we hold fast to God, we are promised blessing (Proverbs 3:18), many years (Deuteronomy 30:20), restoring the years (Joel 2:25), and no one or nothing can stand against us (Deuteronomy 11:22–25)! We will be able to possess bigger and stronger things. Every place we set our feet can be ours. In modern-day terms, blessing will follow us everywhere we go. These same promises of the Old Testament can follow us today and even more since we are under the blood of Jesus. "Jesus Christ is the same yesterday, today, and forever" (Hebrews 13:8 NLT).

One by One

The American Psychological Association also recommends the best way to maintain your goals: "Focus on one goal at a time. The evidence suggests that making a list of New Year's resolutions isn't a great idea. That's because having your willpower become depleted in one realm may reduce willpower in other realms. Instead of trying to adopt better study habits, exercise more and quit smoking all at the same time, take your goals one by one. Once a good habit becomes routine, you no longer need to draw as much on your willpower to maintain it." We set ourselves up for disappointment when we make goals that we do not have the willpower to accomplish. Focusing on one goal—a smaller goal first—will help you reach completion. Then, when you have established that habit, when you are responsible for that thing, you are ready to tackle more.

God's Word teaches us that if we are faithful in the

little things, we'll be faithful in the big things. We'll be ready to pursue bigger goals.

Dave Ramsey, America's most trusted voice of wisdom on finance, teaches the debt snowball method. It's tackling your debt from smallest to largest. What if we used the same approach for any goal? Putting goals in order from smallest to largest and building willpower helps us see the reward of our labor.

If you're struggling with follow-through, focusing on a smaller task first will help you to have more confidence and diligence for the bigger tasks. In the same way, when we see a breakthrough in one area, it always affects our faith in other areas. When the impossible is made possible, even in one area, our faith can be stirred to invite the miraculous in every area. It creates an expectation.

Ears of Expectation

Expectation is powerful. Henry Ford said, "Whether you think you can, or you think you can't—you're right." Your thoughts and your words have an effect on your outcome. Faith comes to change your circumstance, but faith comes by hearing (Romans 10:17). What are you hearing? Are you hearing more about failures or miracles? What you entertain, you feed. And what you feed grows. However, faith can also leave if you're hearing doubt and failure all the time. Our confidence grows one victory at a time. If we're not hearing the Word of God and feeding our spirit, faith can leave one disappointment at a time.

There was a situation where I didn't see any possible

turnaround anymore. I had exerted all the energy, faith, and prayers I could for that circumstance. I believed for a very long time to see change. I thought surely the situation would have resolved by that point. But it wasn't, and I finally reached a point where I was going to give in and settle.

That day, I decided I was just going to pout and bear it until my season changed. The truth is, though, I was already pouting because I didn't believe it truly would change. I complained for a very long time that day. I complained to the extent that I was embarrassed. There was not enough light in the situation for me to see my way out. But, you know what? All was not lost. God saw the way out. He made a way out of "no way" the very next day after I complained so horribly.

God made a miracle happen for me! This is why we must not give up: God is always moving and working in our lives. Even when we can't see the way, He never loses sight of anything. He is about to make a way of escape for us (1 Corinthians 10:13)!

Open to His Possibilities

Holding fast is clinging to God. It's clinging to His Word and clinging to wisdom. Holding fast is meant to protect your heart. It keeps your heart open to the right things, and it guards against hope deferred. If you are not careful, you will think that guarding your heart means maintaining complete control. Guarding your heart is not about guarding against hurt and disappointment. It is about placing your trust in the Lord and yielding to His wisdom that protects you. For me, this meant that I needed to open my heart to His possibilities.

A hardened heart is a sure way to experience hope deferred. It expects disappointment. It is ready for hardship. It looks to the past to foresee trouble. But an open heart knows that it is more important to have a small rearview mirror for the past and a big windshield to look toward the future in hope.

Don't let your hope be deferred. Wait and see. Declare out of your mouth who your God is. Let others know in whom you trust.

I want to encourage you to look at Hebrews 11:6 again. "But without faith it is impossible to please Him, for he who comes to God must believe that He is, and that He is a rewarder of those who diligently seek Him" (NKJV). For a long time, I thought I already knew this verse by heart, but I would leave off the last part. Coming to God in faith does not just require us to believe that God is. We must also believe that He is a rewarder of those who earnestly seek Him.

If you are in a season of holding fast, you must renew your belief that God is a rewarder of those who diligently seek Him. Do not harden your heart and let your hope be deferred. God sees your faith, and He is moving on your behalf! It's safe to trust the Lord. He is your constant. He is your intercessor. He is the One who has your hand when there is uncertainty all around you. He holds you steady.

The reality of your promise is surer than the reality of your present moment. This means that the promises of heaven's realm are more real than what you have yet experienced. I do things every day that don't make sense. How am I—weak as my body is—able to overcome the odds? I shouldn't physically be able to walk and function with the most basic motor skills. Cerebral Palsy is a "chronic, lifelong condition that affects communication between the brain and muscles."[6] Research shows that the underlying brain damage in cerebral palsy is not reversible. However, *incurable* is not a word in God's vocabulary because of Jesus.

Sometimes, when I walk to a meeting or activity, a thought just pops up in my mind: "Wow. I'm really doing this. Praise God." And then, other days, I fall. We all fall in one way or another on occasion. It hurts, and the enemy wants us to question everything. Falling is not failure. It's simply another chance to get up and try again.

Do you feel like you've failed at something? Do you feel as if you're in a valley and can't seem to get up? Are you facing the unknown and seeing fear's ugly, dark face? Don't give up in the shadow of something greater. Press on to see it. It's worth fighting for. Keeping your eyes on the vision is vitally important as you walk past the wilderness. In every season, hold fast to the Word of God. In the valleys and on the mountaintops, create an environment that is conducive for your harvest. There is more to come if you persist in the ways of the Lord. Let's walk with the Lord and inherit the promise.

Waiting in the Word

Abraham held fast for twenty-five years. Everything around him declared that having a son would be impossible for him because his wife, Sarah, was past the age of childbearing in the eyes of the world. I think we can all agree that God thinks very differently than we do. His thoughts are beyond our ability to comprehend every time. We need the Holy Spirit to help us to really understand the things of God. God chose to declare what was humanly impossible over Abraham and Sarah as possible. He declared there were going to be generations and nations birthed through them.

In the same way, Elijah held to the Word of God even when there was no evidence of rain. He trusted the things of the spirit more than the natural. He trusted God's voice enough to keep believing and to keep expecting in the midst of the impossible. It had not rained in three years, but on that day, Elijah had faith for abundant rain. And, the seventh time he sent a servant to look at the sky, there was a small cloud.

What is impossible for you? What do you view as past the realm of possibility for yourself? Maybe you know of others who walk in that possibility but you have a hard time believing it for yourself. What is the mountain you face? I believe God wants to be invited into every part of your life, even in the painful areas, and declare new possibilities.

Take a firm grip on this hope. God's hand is extended to you. Even if you can't see in front of you, God will guide you. Trust Him.

Waiting on His Promises

As I was preparing to graduate from college, my internship at a nonprofit dear to my heart was coming to an end. Interning with this ministry was a fulfillment of a dream, and I didn't want to see it end. I wanted my career path to continue by serving this ministry. I did not have another job lined up, and I wondered what God had ahead. I knew He could see the desires of my heart, but I could not see where He was leading me. I was in the dark about my future. One day, I had a vision of God taking me by the hand and going ahead of me and leading me out of this dark tunnel. God was my sight in that tunnel, and He led me to where He wanted to go, even though I could not see.

God is constantly guiding us and making pathways for us, His children. He is so kind. Jesus was fully man and fully God, so He is aware of our human emotions. He knows what it's like to feel the weight of the world on our shoulders. But this burden is no longer ours to bear because of His finished work on the cross.

God knows that uncertainty makes us nervous. But He also knows that leaning fully on Him will deepen our walk of trust. Remember, at the age of twenty, the Lord asked me a question that changed the course of my life: "Do you trust me?" It took me from a path of putting my certainty on the things of this world to putting my certainty fully and completely on the Lord and His faithfulness.

I answered in my heart, "Yes, Lord, I trust You." I

have not touched my crutches since that day. I had a holy confidence to walk with Him.

I've spiritually walked hand in hand with the Lord every day, and many times, I've walked hand in hand physically with those around me. Taking a leap of faith and trust in Him has not been easy by any means. It often baffles those around me why I don't use my crutches. Sometimes people ask, "Wouldn't it be easier to go back? Why not go back to the old way?" (As I'm sure you know, not everyone will understand your journey. That's okay.) The people of Israel asked a similar question (paraphrasing): "Wouldn't it be easier to go back to Egypt where there was food?" It seems humanly safe to turn back—there is comfort in the familiar.

But, in the words of Mr. Beaver from *The Chronicles of Narnia*, "Safe? ... Who said anything about safe? 'Course he isn't safe. But he's good. He's the King, I tell you." [7]

I'm not looking for earthly safety or even comfort, I'm looking for a heavenly inheritance! There's more to life than what our natural eyes can see. I've seen just a glimpse of what holy abandon to God's call can do, and there's a greater promise ahead for those of us who don't turn back. We don't have to understand why to be obedient to God's leading. As a result of this journey, I have seen abiding reassurance of my favorite scripture (Psalm 46:1 NIV): "God is our refuge and strength, an ever-present help in trouble." Oh, how present He is with us! He sends just what we need at the right time. His attention to the details of our lives is breathtaking.

He has proven His faithfulness again and again on my journey to walk without crutches. Just like this timeworn hymn says, "Tis so sweet to trust in Jesus, Just to take Him at His word; Just to rest upon His promise; Just to know, Thus saith the Lord. Jesus, Jesus, how I trust Him, How I've proved Him o'er and o'er, Jesus, Jesus, Precious Jesus! O for grace to trust Him more."[8]

I believe you are going to experience His faithfulness like never before in your life when you trust in Him with abandon! This journey of walking in obedience to what God says is going to open every door. But there's still more to talk about before you can hold fast to hope with a firm grip.

I remember three things the Lord promised me when I began this journey. I am walking in the first promise, and the other two will come in time. When these promises were given to me, my spirit was stirred with faith, and I received them.

Everyone has promises that the Lord wants to give them. Promises are all throughout His Word. The question is, do you know what they are? We absolutely can have everything His Word says, but God also wants to speak to us individually. He created us, and He knows how to fulfill our purpose. He knows how to guide us.

Yes, the promises God gives us are desirable and amazing! They are always better than any dream we could dream of. But not only are the promises of God better than a dream come true; they fulfill a divine purpose! When God promises you something, you can guarantee that He will use it for His glory! That's why I am so passionate about seeing God's promises fulfilled—God gets the glory!

Let's explore what God has promised you in His Word. Everything God has we have access to, because we are children of God!

- God is with us (Joshua 1:9).
- God is for us (John 3:16).
- We have an invitation to His presence (Psalm 100:4).
- Goodness and mercy follow us (Psalm 23:6).
- Peace is ours for the taking (Philippians 4:6–7).
- God invites us to surrender every burden (Matthew 11:28).
- We have authority to access God's will on earth (Matthew 16:19).

This just skims the surface of promises available to every believer. Only you know the personal promises God has for you. Only you and your Creator know the deepest longings of your heart. Seek Him and hold fast to the vision He gives you for your life. In Habakkuk 2:2–3, we see that Habakkuk was commanded to write the vision God gave Him and make it plain so that it can be read on the run. Let's run with the promises of God!

The promises God has for us are worth the journey! The impossibilities you have seen in the past cannot hinder you from where God is taking you. You are going to enter a new place of victory once you decide to walk into it. God leads us through the process into His promises. He is not slow in fulfilling them. He will finish what He starts (2 Peter 3:9, Philippians 1:6).

Isaiah 40:31 holds the key to God's promise of renewed strength. It's not in our own ability to hold on that makes us strong; it's what we hold on to. We step into God's plan by taking His hand. I know that I am not strong enough to hold on—in my own strength. I have to rely on God's grace and truth. There will be times when we think about quitting. There will be times when we are convinced we can't go on. It's important to fill up on fresh hope when discouragement, disappointment, and disillusionment knock. Waiting is not easy, but it's worth it.

So what is the promise in Isaiah 40:31? "But those who hope in the Lord will renew their strength. They will soar on wings like eagles; they will run and not grow weary, they will walk and not be faint" (NIV).

Wait and hope in the Lord, not strength, and your strength will be renewed! Sometimes it feels as if we need fresh strength to tackle things and get a firm grip on what we want to see happen. But our human efforts to increase strength won't last as long as the strength God provides. Hope in Him first, and watch what He does in your life! What you once could only hope for will be fulfilled in front of you!

When you acknowledge the ways God fulfills His personal promises to you, others are drawn to God's mighty and faithful hand. By now, are you beginning to see a greater glimpse of what He has promised you? Take time to write down what He puts on your heart.

Then, let only God receive the glory for what He has done! He who promised is faithful! Again, I will declare: "Let us hold unswervingly to the hope we profess, for He who promised is faithful" (Hebrews 10:23 NIV). Oh, so faithful!

PART TWO ━━━━

The Journey

— FOUR —

Walk in Thankfulness

Rejoice in the Lord always. I will say it again: Rejoice!

—Philippians 4:4 (NIV)

Rejoicing can go a long way. It creates a positive atmosphere for God to work. It also promotes thankfulness. In any circumstance, thankfulness is a catalyst for God to receive glory. A thankful vantage point causes us to be able to see more everyday miracles. Rejoicing not only benefits us, but it also benefits others.

Kyran is a gentleman who understands the power of thankfulness and positivity. Kyran works on airport runways every day. He is one of the many workers who help airline passengers have a successful flight. But there is something that sets Kyran apart from his coworkers. In fact, you may have seen Kyran before. A happy passenger caught footage that went viral of Kyran dancing on the tarmac.

Rather than treating his job as ordinary, Kyran goes above and beyond to make this airline's passengers smile.

He says, "If I can just do something so small just to turn your day around, give you just a smile, to get ready to start your day, then I've done my job."[9]

Kyran sees his job description differently than most, and because of his unique perspective, he is able to lift the spirits of many. I want to be more like Kyran! I want to seize every moment to spread joy. It's so easy to get caught up in everyday routines. Without thought, we slip into the mundane and often joyless normal. It takes effort to think differently, but it's scientifically proven that we can create new pathways of thinking in our brains. I'm so grateful that we don't have to be stuck in old patterns! We can choose joy. We can choose to rejoice.

Kyran isn't above human struggle; he just chooses joy because that is what he wants to share with the world. We aren't above struggle either, but we can see a shift in ourselves and others when we choose to rejoice in all circumstances. "Rejoice always, pray continually, give thanks in all circumstances; for this is God's will for you in Christ Jesus" (1 Thessalonians 5:16–18 NIV).

Giving thanks in all circumstances helps us to fulfill our callings. As you know, all circumstances means every one of them, whether you judge it to be good or bad. Become someone who recognizes the silver lining! If you need provision, give thanks that you know Jehovah Jireh— our provider. If you need healing, thank God you know He is Jehovah Rapha—our healer. If you need peace, give thanks, because your God is Jehovah Shalom over you!

We are never alone, and that is something be overjoyed about. We are not going to feel like rejoicing all the time. It's tough some days. What I'm most excited to show you, though, is how rejoicing can turn your situation around. Rejoicing is more than a good thought. Rejoicing actually has power to release what you ask for.

Meet in The Middle

I was eight years old when I first learned that God can meet you in the middle of your circumstance. I had just been released from the hospital after a week of recovery from a major surgery to improve my gait. I was on heavy pain killers all week to manage the pain of the surgery. If you know me, you know it doesn't take much for me to get loopy. I laugh all the time anyway, and the anesthesia for surgery really affects me. It takes a while for it to wear off, and I get nauseated. With anesthetic, I am twice as giggly. I would've been the life of the party if it wasn't for the nausea and the pain.

But after I went home, from the hospital, all the strong pain relievers were gone, and my smiles were, too. I remember feeling such a heaviness hit my little eight-year-old body. All the medicine had worn off. My body was writhing in pain. I couldn't do anything but scream. I screamed out to Jesus, "Jesus, make it stop!" My mom says now that she was proud of me for knowing whom to call, yet she was sad I was in so much pain. The only way I know how to describe the feeling is like a mix between withdrawal shivers and shooting, throbbing, excruciating aches. It still makes my hair stand up on end to think about it. I felt so helpless in that moment.

Praise God the Holy Spirit led my dad to do something that has marked my life to this day. He put on praise and worship music and called down heaven for me. It was my first memory of tangible victory. After lingering in that moment, worshipping and praying, there was a peace that came into the room. It was as if peace just entered through the door and walked over to my bed. The Holy Spirit was invited into my time of need. I experienced a tangible difference in my body. I know now that God delivered me from the pain. He exchanged it for an indescribable calm. I went from feeling locked in a prison of pain in my body to a release in a miraculous instant. It was like my whole body had been tense, and when the pain finally let go, I could relax and breathe.

God is always *with us*. But when we praise and worship God, we are *with Him*. We can enter heaven's gates with praise and thanksgiving. "Enter his gates with thanksgiving and his courts with praise; give thanks to him and praise his name" (Psalm 100:4 NIV). We are the ones who have to make a conscious choice to be present with Him—to acknowledge Him and invite Him in. When we call, God moves into another level of action for us. My eight-year-old cry was an invitation. My worship, and my parents' worship, was an invitation. It was an invitation for God to meet us right in the middle of our pain. I will never forget that He heard my cry that day. "But in my distress I cried out to the Lord; yes, I prayed to my God for help. He heard me from his sanctuary; my cry to him reached his ears" (Psalm 18:6 NLT).

Praise and worship is the best way to invite God's

presence into your situation. It's where the despair of your circumstance and the joy of our Sovereign Lord meet in the middle. The moment my pain left, it was like someone just lifted it off of me. Or, maybe it just got swallowed up in peace. Whatever pain or distress you may need to be swallowed up in tangible peace today, please know that the Lord hears your cry. With an invitation, there's nothing the Lord can't do.

Cry out to Him, and then turn up the worship. Put on a powerful album or playlist, and let go of your agenda. Surrender, and wait for God's calmness to come over you. God never fails. I promise you, He will meet you in the middle of where you are, because I know He is already there with you. There's nowhere we can go to flee from God, even if we try. He's just waiting on your willingness to invite Him in.

God has delivered me many times, and He has also shown His mighty hand of provision more times than I can remember. I remember an unshakable instance when I first encountered God's financial provision for me. I was fourteen years old, just before my freshman year of high school. I was passionate about Jesus and my youth group more than anything. When it was announced that there was a mission trip for the high schoolers, I asked if I could go.

I don't know what he was thinking, but somehow I must have convinced my youth pastor that I was capable of traveling internationally to the precious nation of El Salvador. Oh my goodness, the hills and the mountains. The high school guys had to carry me up all of the hills and stairs. I think one of them told me that carrying me that week was his way to make up for missing football camp! God just lines up all the details, even conditioning. There's no natural reason why I should have been able to go. God went above and beyond for me. He made sure that my mom could get off work to go with me. He made sure that when I couldn't walk, even with my crutches, that there was someone there to hold my hands or carry me. Looking back, that seems like a lot of effort just to make sure a girl with a disability could be a part of "go and make disciples …" (Matthew 28:19 NIV).

Our limits are no match for God. If He tells you to go, go! From experience, I know He delights in making a way for you. He delights in making the impossible possible. He delights in your gratitude. There were so many reasons why I could have stayed back. I could have said, "No, I can't." And, if I had, it probably would have looked reasonable. But there was a desire in me to go, and, I decided to test the limits. To follow God and see what happened.

Besides the physical limitations, I had to trust God financially as well. I remember the day of the deadline came for fundraising, and I still needed a big chunk of money. I don't remember what led me to do it (probably my dad and memories of tangible victory in worship), but I cried out to God and thanked Him in advance for meeting my need. I let the praise and worship music blare, and I had such a good time. I could just feel the Lord's presence. I was more aware of His nearness. Then

I got the call: "Your balance is paid in full! You're going to El Salvador!"

Praise the Lord not only for the times when He meets our needs financially, but when He meets needs we didn't even know we had. I wasn't aware of how badly I needed to know that I could be a part of answering the call. I didn't realize how much I needed to grow in compassion. I didn't have the slightest idea how a trip could affect my life. We all have a calling, a purpose, on our lives. The enemy would like nothing more than to keep us from discovering it. And, if he can't keep us in the dark, he will give us excuses. "You can't because …" "What about …?" If I had not pushed away the questions with praise, I wouldn't be where I am today. I challenge you to push back excuses and doubt with praise! Heaven will move on your behalf.

Praise into Purpose

Fast forward a few years, to when I was eighteen. I had graduated high school with a perfect GPA, but I had no practical idea what I was going to do with my life. For some reason, I let the limits of my body limit my future. I hadn't given up; I just didn't know what to do. The only thing I knew at the time was that the structure of school was what I excelled at. So, for me, I thought the best step would be to go to college.

I felt so clueless those first few months of college as to my life's purpose. I knew I wanted to help people. When I thought about it, I would always go back to the same accusing belief. "What am I really going to be able to do?" Part of me didn't believe in myself. I wanted so much more, but I thought I was going to have to settle.

If you have trouble dreaming about your future, as I did, it may be because you don't want to get your hopes up. When you awaken to your purpose, you have to let your hopes up! Your purpose is God ordained. Don't let your self-doubt argue with God. Worship is what awakened me to my purpose.

One day, I was at church, and we had a special guest speaker. I had never seen or heard this preacher, and I don't think I have since. After the preaching, we had another time of worship. I walked up to the altar with my crutches, and I just stood there in awe of God. As I worshipped, the guest speaker had me brought over to him. He told me, "There's something special about you." He repeated, "There's something special about you." He had my attention now. He continued, "Do you know who Mephibosheth is in the Bible? God wants you to see yourself in a new way. Not for the inadequacies, but that God has made a place for you at His table even now." The same is true for all of us.

Even now, even in the midst of our mess, even in the midst of our need, even in the midst of our weakness and limitations—God has a place for us. God used the words of that preacher to awaken me to God's plan. God's plan wasn't for me to settle. God's place for me was at His table. When I should have been disqualified in the world's eyes, God called me to participate in what He was doing. God called me to sit with Him!

That moment was the confirmation I needed to let my hopes up! I needed to dream. I needed to obey. I just needed a reminder of the power of worship. In my worship, God answered me by bringing His mighty and royal invitation to me!

Your praise will bring you into your purpose. Don't keep your head down. Raise your head. Lift your eyes and declare God's goodness. You might just walk into your divine purpose the next time you turn on "Every Praise!"[10]

Cleared for Take-Off

> Be anxious for nothing, but in everything by prayer and supplication, with thanksgiving, let your requests be made known to God; and the peace of God, which surpasses all understanding, will guard your hearts and minds through Christ Jesus.
>
> —Philippians 4:6–7 (NKJV)

When we present our requests to God with thanksgiving, His peace is promised to follow us and guard us. God's peace guards our minds and helps us to be in alignment with His will. As we guard our minds, we realize that God's way of thinking is so much higher than ours. "For as the heavens are higher than the earth, So are My ways higher than your ways, And My thoughts than your thoughts" (Isaiah 55:9 NKJV). God's thoughts are on a higher level. They soar above our own. If God's thoughts are so much higher, and if He guards our minds, we should consider that a ticket to soar a little higher.

We are to take captive every thought and make it obedient to Christ (see 2 Corinthians 10:5).

Remember Kyran, the tarmac dancer? I think he may already have that ticket—the ticket to soar to a higher level of thinking.

Joy takes us higher. Praise takes us higher. It lifts our heads to see God's perspective. When you are waiting to see God come through, pray and count it all joy. "Count it all joy, my brothers, when you meet trials of various kinds, for you know that the testing of your faith produces steadfastness. And let steadfastness have its full effect, that you may be perfect and complete, lacking in nothing" (James 1:2–4 ESV).

It was and is my joy to be considered fit for the King's table. Is there something that you think disqualifies you? Whatever it is, God is ready for your praise and your willingness even now.

Not only was Mephibosheth a lame man invited to the King's table, he always ate there. His identity was no longer in what he lacked but rather the life-changing opportunity he had. Mephibosheth was taken care of and provided for throughout the rest of his life, like royalty.

> "Don't be afraid," David said to him, "for I will surely show you kindness for the sake of your father Jonathan. I will restore to you all the land that belonged to your

grandfather Saul, and you will always eat at my table." Mephibosheth bowed down and said, "What is your servant, that you should notice a dead dog like me?" Then the king summoned Ziba, Saul's steward, and said to him, "I have given your master's grandson everything that belonged to Saul and his family. You and your sons and your servants are to farm the land for him and bring in the crops, so that your master's grandson may be provided for. And Mephibosheth, grandson of your master, will always eat at my table." (Now Ziba had fifteen sons and twenty servants.) Then Ziba said to the king, "Your servant will do whatever my lord the king commands his servant to do." So Mephibosheth ate at David's table like one of the king's sons" (2 Samuel 9:7–11 NIV).

Your place at the King's table is not in question. You are a son or daughter of the King! Get used to His provision. Get comfortable in His presence. You are going to spend a lot of time with Him.

With Mephibosheth held in the high regard of Prince now, He had more access to the King. But he did not let familiarity get in the way of honor. Mephibosheth honored King David for both his position of authority and for all he had done in his life.

We, like Mephibosheth, need to honor the King of Kings any time we get the chance. We are His children, and we get to be with Him a lot, but let's not forget the basics of how to enter a King's presence: thanksgiving.

Praise comes before a victory in God's Kingdom. God shouts and walls come down. When we follow His lead, we see victory. Praise allows God to fight the battle. Rejoicing in a trial does not diminish what you're going through; it just opens the door for God to move.

Praise gets the attention of the Lord quicker than anything else. It summons His presence. It reminds us that we are seated with Him in victory. Our praise enthrones God.

The Exchange

Praise is to exchange our heaviness. It is not a byproduct of joy; praise literally brings joy. Whatever belief you have held about why you can't worship and praise God, I dare you to step outside of that stronghold. Step out of the heaviness. Step out of the darkness and into the light with your praise.

God anointed Jesus to rescue us. He brings victory where there is defeat. "To console those who mourn in Zion, To give them beauty for ashes, The oil of joy for mourning, The garment of praise for the spirit of heaviness; That they may be called trees of righteousness, The planting of the LORD, that He may be glorified" (Isaiah 61:3 NKJV)

With God we do not have to stay permanently in mourning. Because we are at God's table, our cups run over. In God's presence, we can overflow with divine joy. He is the One who anoints our heads with oil. The oil of joy calls us from where we are to where He is.

I challenge you to give God your ashes and let Him turn it into beauty. Give God your mourning, so He can exchange it for you. Give God everything so that nothing hinders your praise.

Lift your voice. Mark this season. You have to step out of this season to move on to the next. We have to start each new journey right: with thanksgiving and praise. Heaviness is no more when praise fills our mouths with songs of victory.

Praise leads the front lines of battle because we trust our God. No matter what the situation looks like, we trust our God. The Israelites were excited and full of praise for their newfound freedom out of Egypt, but as soon as hardship came, they exchanged their praise for murmuring and complaining.

Unfortunately, it's easy to do. One minute we can say, "I will rejoice and be glad because this is the day the Lord has made" (see Psalm 118:24). Then, the next moment or hour, we get a phone call with bad news, and naturally, we complain. "Isn't this awful?" The decision to meditate on the bad ruins our entire day. The Israelites focused on the negatives for so long that it seemed as if they had forgotten all God had done for them. They complained about everything, so they forgot why they left the bondage of captivity.

> And the children of Israel said to them, "Oh, that we had died by the hand of the LORD in the land of Egypt, when we sat by the pots of meat and when we ate bread to the full! For you have brought us out into this wilderness to kill this whole assembly with hunger." Then the LORD said to Moses, "Behold, I will rain bread from heaven for you. And the people shall go out and gather a certain quota every day, that I may test them, whether they will walk in My law or not. (Exodus 16:3–4 NKJV)

Hunger makes me more apt to complain. I've been "hangry" before (so hungry that you're angry). The Israelites were hangry. They were tired. They thought they had been through enough. They talked so much about food that God finally responded with the provision of manna, bread from heaven.

God had an order for the Israelites' journey, and He has one for each of us, too. God will respond even in the midst of our complaints, but how much more He would respond to our trust and praise?

God can orchestrate things in a way that leaves no question about who has made a way for you. It is by Him alone that you are still here, and for that reason alone, He deserves your eternal thanks. There was no other way that the Israelites could have had manna provided for them. Literally no one had ever seen it before! They had to ask, "What is it?" when they saw it. Moses was able to tell them it was bread from heaven—provision from God.

There is no question in my mind that God has made a way for you. It's how He operates. If you ever find yourself asking, "What is this? What is going on?" know you are not alone, but that God's provision is greater than what you can see. He is making a way for you—whatever you need! So, offer your thanks to God knowing He has everything under control. Praise Him knowing He inhabits the praises of His people! Let's enthrone Him every chance we get (see Psalm 22:3).

Steadfast in Praise

You won't always feel like praising even though you know it's the right thing to do. When I am facing hardships one after another, my praise is a sacrifice. I would dare to say that when we praise God when things are difficult, it brings Him the most glory. It shows God that our hearts are proven in sincerity. Are you willing to offer a sacrifice of praise? Are you willing to abandon your understanding of your situation for the sake of giving God glory?

The scriptures tells us to lean not to our own understanding in Proverbs 3:5–6 (NIV): "Trust in the Lord with all your heart and lean not on your own understanding; in all your ways submit to him, and he will make your paths straight." We must learn to lean not on our own assessments, but to submit to God's understanding.

We cannot always fully understand His ways, but we can live in a way that acknowledges, "I don't know how this will work out, but God knows. Therefore, I choose to trust and praise Him, and He will direct my way."

The hardest times for me to worship are when I am sick in my body or sick with grief. But those are times I need to worship the most. I need it, because it ushers in His presence of peace and comfort. There are times when I literally cannot take a step without offering Him praise. I know it's not by my might, ability, or power that I move. "Not by might nor by power, but by my Spirit, says the Lord Almighty" (Zechariah 4:6 NIV). He is the one Who is with me every step of the way.

There are also times I cannot move without reminding myself of God's truth. I wish I could adequately describe the "pause" that comes along with palsy. Some moments my brain freezes and will not communicate with my leg muscles. It makes it seem impossible to move, to continue on this journey of walking. But, when the "pause" comes, I stop and regroup. I quote scriptures or declarations (some might call them affirmations). Or, sometimes, I will say to myself, "Sarah, God didn't say stop." And sometimes I pray for help. It always comes in one way or another. Sometimes, I am able to "press play" in my brain and continue walking, and other times, God sends an angel. Some are gracious friends at the right moment, and sometimes it's more mysterious than that. Somehow, someway, I move forward as if with a hand on my back guiding me. I've often wondered how many angels it takes to keep me safe!

I have to continually partner with God and what He says about me. My body is quick to remind me of my insufficiency. So, I have to renew my mind with a higher authority. There is no higher, more righteous word of authority than God's Word. That's why I choose to affirm myself with scripture and declare what He says. It helps me stay in a mindset of praise.

I praise God that in Him, I am strong. In Him, I have abundant life. In Him, I can climb any mountain. In Him, I am able. In Christ, I can do all things (see Philippians 4:13). The only thing I can compare the "pause" to is to the way that fear cripples any of us. Fear is no respecter of persons. Fear would like to torment all of us. But it's something we can push past with a higher authority of truth. When fear tells me, "You can't," Philippians 4:13 is one of my favorite verses to quote. You cannot think something into being; you have to follow through on the idea. That's why I don't just think positive thoughts—I speak them. I don't just think about praising God—I speak it from my heart out of my mouth.

Our rejoicing can be our greatest weapon. The enemy does not understand genuine praise in times of adversity. When we are careful to respond with praise, the enemy can't stand it. It thwarts his plans and intentions. It catapults us into God's will!

When you feel beaten down by life, take it as a compliment. The devil is throwing all he can your way to divert your attention. When this happens, proceed with caution. You are in danger of contaminating your steadfast spirit with your own words. Resist the temptation to complain. Please hear me—I am not saying we do not need to be authentic, transparent and vulnerable. But guard yourself against creating a negative mindset.

Complaining opens the door to something much worse: discouragement. If you make a habit of complaining, you'll discourage yourself with your own mouth. The angel told Clarence in the classic Christmas movie *It's a Wonderful Life* that the main character, George Bailey, needed heaven's help. The help George needed wasn't for sickness or bodily trouble. The angel said it was worse than sickness: "He's discouraged."[11]

Discouragement is serious! Watch what you let entertain your ears, and watch what you say. If you complain, you'll discourage yourself.

Rather than beat yourself down, encourage yourself! Moses was told to encourage Joshua (see Deuteronomy 1:38), and we're told to encourage each other. "Therefore encourage one another and build each other up, just as in fact you are doing" (1 Thessalonians 5:11 NIV).

We need to inherit what God has promised us. We can't inherit with a negative mindset! The next time you're tempted to complain, remember what's at stake and encourage yourself and those around you. We are able to thrive when we have support and accountability.

God is with us throughout our entire journey. Do not lose sight or be deceived if things get hard. He is with you, and His heart is for you to come into greater faith and promise. Pain and trials are fleeting. They seem all-consuming, but they are not!

I recall a time I had leg casts taken off. The process of having the casts taken off scared me, but the removal process did not hurt. What hurt were the metal pins that were yanked out of my feet without any numbing! Ouch! It was time for these pins to come out because they were no longer useful. Yet, it was extremely painful. I screamed out in agony and almost cut off someone's blood flow from squeezing them too hard (sorry, Mom). But the end result was good. Agony and pain do not last. Be at peace and know that pain it is only a moment in time.

God's instruction to "rejoice at all times" or "rejoice always" is not to mock a difficult period or season. God's encouragement for us to rejoice actually keeps us strong and fit for His promise to us. If you have not experienced fullness of joy, then you have not yet recognized or experienced the fullness of God's abiding presence (see Psalm 16:11). His presence carries us through setbacks. When having a hard time rejoicing, be still and know He is God until you can lift up praise (see Psalm 46:10).

When I learned how to read the Bible as a little girl, the first verse of Psalm 46 was my favorite: "God is our refuge and strength, an ever-present help in trouble" (NIV). Can you tell that this passage is still very special to me? God has proven to be the ever-present help I need. He's always there. He never fails. God doesn't promise us trouble-free zones, but He shows us that we are strong because His is with us.

Rejoicing quickens us to keep our eyes on the Ever-Present One. Rejoicing is much more than saying good things. When thankfulness and rejoicing are a lifestyle, it is a prophetic declaration of victory before we see it.

So, rejoice. Prophesy. Praise. Take a step in the right direction knowing God is with you, and He will give you all you need to be victorious. Don't stay stuck in a painful or difficult moment in time. Praise your way into the promise. Invite Him into your every moment—your joy and your pain.

> Therefore, having been justified by faith, we have peace with God through our Lord Jesus Christ, through whom also we have access by faith into this grace in which we stand, and rejoice in hope of the glory of God. And not only that, but we also glory in tribulations, knowing that tribulation produces perseverance; and perseverance, character; and character, hope. Now hope does not disappoint, because the love of God has been poured out in our hearts by the Holy Spirit who was given to us. (Romans 5:1–5 NKJV)

God is the One we must seek to walk steadfastly in His powerful hope. We will not be disappointed when our hope is in Him. With our hearts fixed on trusting and praising the Lord, we are ready to begin the journey!

FIVE

Walk by Faith

*For we walk by faith, not by sight [living
our lives in a manner consistent with our
confident belief in God's promises].*

—2 Corinthians 5:7 (AMP)

The Gift

Faith gives us access to what we cannot see. It's a key to
unlock heaven in our lives. And when we use the keys
God has given us consistently (steadfastly), we will realize
that no good thing is withheld from us. God holds us in
His hands—He is most careful with us. And I believe the
angels hold assignments of blessings in their hands.

Your faith is a key that activates heaven. I can see a
picture of God giving instruction to the angels. With a
firm grip, they hold the next blessing assigned to come
our way, and it's the thing we've been fervently praying
for. It's wrapped like an elegant gift. The angel I picture is
using both of his hands to hold the blessing. One hand is

holding the bottom, and the other is covering the top as if concealing a precious surprise. When the appointed time comes, the angel will open his hand to let the blessing pour out over us.

I believe there are three things that God showed me regarding the angels' instructions to release blessings and answers to prayer over us. The first type of instruction is to release them when we ask! How simple is that? I love that God clearly tells His children in His Word that we can ask.

> Ask and it will be given to you; seek and you will find; knock and the door will be opened to you. For everyone who asks receives; the one who seeks finds; and to the one who knocks, the door will be opened. (Matthew 7:7–8 NIV)

The second type of instruction is for blessings to be released when we pass tests. (Yes, tests, trials, and sufferings are good for us. They build our perseverance, character, and ultimately our hope in God (see Romans 5:1–5)). I believe the third and final type of instruction God allowed me to see is the one that perplexes our human minds the most. Blessings are to be released at an appointed time! The appointed time both mystifies and anchors our faith journey. God is sovereign. Those who walk in faith will not be afraid to *wait*. They know God is moving, and He never forgets His children.

If you could only see the instruction God gives the angels! What we're praying for is not far off and forgotten in heaven. It's being carefully placed in the hands of the angels. Your time is coming! It's here! God knows the perfect time and season to send the rain, and He knows the proper time to release heaven over you.

I pray this gives you assurance that there's more than what meets the eye. Faith is a *gift*, according to 1 Corinthians 12:9. Everyone has a least some measure of faith (Romans 12:3). The good thing is that you don't need to have a lot of faith to move the heart of God. You just have to have faith as tiny as a seed, and that seed will tackle mountains (Matthew 17:20 MSG).

The Lord knew I would need a lot of faith for this journey I'm on. I pray for my faith to stir others, but it still baffles me why it's often so easy for my faith gift to rise up while others focus on fear. Don't get me wrong; I've been fearful at times, but for some reason, my faith is always stronger than the fear, doubt, or worry. Often times, I wonder if He gave me an extra helping of faith. (In the south, that means "more on our plate," or another round of food.)

I think God gives us all a good measure, and He doesn't limit us either! We can ask for more (see James 1:5), and we have the ability to grow what He gives us. God's gifts grow, increase, and multiply with the Word! "So then faith *comes* by hearing, and hearing by the word of God" (Romans 10:17 NKJV).

When I was a child, I didn't start out with the faith I have now. For everyone, the gift of faith starts out small, and it grows and matures over time. We need to water our faith with the Word of God. Routinely. We can't just water a seed or a plant one time and hope it lasts.

We have to be intentional and create an environment conducive for it to grow.

Connect It

Faith is a substance (see Hebrews 11:1). It's a real thing, but it does not see with natural eyes. Faith sees with spiritual eyes. When my faith sees something as possible, it's a sure thing. I know that I know that I *know* it's going to happen. Have you ever experienced that?

When that sense of faith is stirred up so strong, I usually know it's going to take a while to see it happen in the natural, but in the spirit realm God has already given me the answer. Something I love to do is to put my faith into action. I love to buy things in faith. For example, if I'm agreeing in prayer for something, sometimes I'll purchase something as an action of faith. Most often, it's a gift for someone else, like a baby item for my friends believing to get pregnant. It's like you're speaking it into existence. At home, I display reminders on my vision board as an act of faith, or I stick Post-it notes around the office that inspire my faith.

Faith is fun when you have your spiritual eyes open. You're seeing things in a different light. Walking by faith is not walking blindly; it's choosing to believe that there's a bigger picture. My faith loves not only walking but jumping out of airplanes! God is with us, and I believe He wants to invite us into a different realm of living. Where faith is our most valuable commodity—it's our ticket to a life of great adventure. Why let your feet stay on the ground if you can soar?

Let's Say Yes to Adventure

I went skydiving for the first time in 2018. Skydiving was so freeing for me. I felt as though I no longer had any limitations. *The sky* was not even the limit. I was moving swiftly through the air on top of the world. The level of joy I experienced felt like being on cloud nine. Literally, I guess!

It was just me, the instructor, God, and a parachute—18,000 feet in the air. It was heavenly. I wanted to go again and again. I got up in the airplane, and I wasn't scared. I was thrilled! Adventure can seem nerve-wracking, but it also awakens something in us. It awakens a desire to live a radically different life. Let's say *yes* more often and *no* to worry and stress. As I type this, I hear an airplane flying by, and I can't help but smile. Let's keep saying *yes* to His adventures for our lives!

Armor

Faith is also described as a shield that protects us from all the flaming arrows of the evil one. Do all you can to hold on to your shield. Use it by reading God's Word, meditating on it, writing it on the tablet of your heart; then you will speak it. Just like your muscles, your faith won't grow if you don't feed it and use it. God's armor clothes us with a confidence we are meant to carry every day.

Activation

Testimonies display God's heart in an incredible way. What God does for one, He can do for others. Testimonies are an invitation for you to see full activation of God's promises in faith. There is more that God has for us! We can walk in miracles. We can see God's faithfulness, because He never changes. He stands by His Word. God initiates His promises and our faith. He perfects our faith, and He completes the promise at the appointed time; it will not prove false (Habakkuk 2:3 NIV).

Jesus, our champion, initiates and perfects our faith. Faith does not come from our own human confidence. It is our supernatural assurance and evidence of what is yet to come. Jesus initiated our faith. And, when He did that, He initiated the sequence of your promise. Do you understand that your promise has already been set in motion? The sequence Jesus started will be completed. It has a set time. Wait for completion. Expect it!

Some believers only have faith for eternal life. Others have a greater measure of faith because they understand the perfect character of God. He not only gives us eternal life, but He tells us that abundant life can start here on earth. Activate your faith now!

Pastor Amanda Crabb says, "Faith is full activation in the heavenlies." Faith activates heaven. It declares, "On earth as it is in heaven" (Matthew 6:10 NIV). If you want to activate heaven on earth, you have to speak the Word of God. Angels hearken to the Word of God.

Testing

Words will be tested. The enemy of our souls would love to steal what God has planted deep within us. Sometimes activating the Word of the Lord—by speaking it, declaring it, and writing it on the tablet of our hearts—seems like a fight. For me, putting these words into a book has proven to be a wrestling match. God's Word is declared in Hebrews 4:12 as "living and powerful, and sharper than any two-edged sword, piercing even to the division of soul and spirit, and of joints and marrow, and is a discerner of the thoughts and intents of the heart" (NKJV). It divides soul and spirit. It brings to light the core of what we believe.

A test or trial of your faith will reveal if your faith will be depleted or strengthened. I have experienced trials, and I know that a test can turn into a testimony. I want to share more than my own experiences. I want to share testimonies of my brothers and sisters in Christ, because their trials strengthened their faith (and mine). I know it can build your faith, too.

Testimonies

Melanie's Testimony

I've seen Melanie wrestle with heartbreaking loss while trying to start a family. Miscarriage seems like it has no closure. Ultimately, Melanie's grief stole all of her strength. She wondered to herself, "Is this how people walk away [from God]?" Melanie felt like she had nothing left in her to survive this. But when Melanie felt hopeless, when her faith was down to its lowest point, that's when God carried her. God fought this battle for her, and I believe Psalm 13 is a good depiction of her heart's cry:

> How long, Lord? Will you forget me forever?
> How long will you hide your face from me?
> How long must I wrestle with my thoughts and day after day have sorrow in my heart?
> How long will my enemy triumph over me?
> Look on me and answer, Lord my God.
> Give light to my eyes, or I will sleep in death,
> and my enemy will say, "I have overcome him,"
> and my foes will rejoice when I fall.
> But I trust in your unfailing love;
> my heart rejoices in your salvation.
> I will sing the Lord's praise,
> for he has been good to me. (NIV)

Melanie overcame this heart-wrenching, dark trial because of the hands of the One who carried her. Her faith was shaken, but still, it remained and was reinforced. She knows she will see her first child again. Her firstborn will grow in strength forever in the Lord's presence. Her first child never knew the brokenness of this world, and I believe the child will be watching closely as his or her family grows on earth.

This is not the end of the story. Instead of running and hiding in fear, Melanie faced fear head-on and continued to believe in faith for children. For some reason, whenever I saw a giraffe toy or giraffe themed nursery decor, the Lord reminded me to pray for Melanie. What she sowed in tears of sorrow, she reaped in tears of joy after she was finally able to give birth to a son. It brought me a lot of joy recently to see Melanie with her son dressed in a giraffe costume. It reminded me that the Lord hears our cries. If you are facing a trial of loss, I pray you will reap tears of joy, too. Allow God and the prayers of others to fight for you. For "we overcome by the blood of the Lamb, and the word of our testimony" (Revelation 12:11 NKJV).

Shane's Testimony

I am so grateful to share part of my cousin Shane's story with you. When I am around him, my joy level multiplies. He can make me belly laugh just by looking at me! We both grew up knowing who Jesus was. But, as a teenager, Shane stopped going to church.

The world grew loud all around him. Voices of doubt became all he could hear without a community of believers around him. I could see that his life was riddled with confusion and chaos. I prayed that he would find his way to God.

Years passed, and even though Shane lived how he wanted to, he knew something was missing. He became desperate to know the truth about God.

Questions flooded his mind, and each one swayed his beliefs like a seesaw. "How can I be certain that what I grew up knowing as fact is true?" He dug deep into history and researched the historical facts and Biblical accounts. His mind began to change. Eventually, Shane was nudged to go on a mission trip to Jamaica.

On the trip, Shane had a wakeup call. He met a young man named Andre. Andre testified that he used to be a gang member and that God changed his life. Now Andre lives for God. Extremely moved by Andre's transformed life, Shane went home from that trip ready for a change in his own life.

For Shane, faith is simple now. He lives to love God and God's people. He knows firsthand just how incredibly patient and loving the Lord is. He knows that God can handle our questions and doubts. He knows that questions don't make God angry with us; He is patiently waiting for us to come to Him.

I'm so grateful the Lord hears our prayers for our loved ones. Don't stop praying. I praise God Shane has his foundation on the rock now. He found his purpose! Shane works for a mission organization alongside his beautiful wife. He gets to see the good news of Christ transcend cultural barriers every day, because every tribe can understand the language of love!

Payne's Testimony

Have you ever been in a trial, and by the grace of God, your faith reassures you that you have victory before you see it? There have been times in a hard situation when I still smile because God reassures my heart that *I have the victory*! God is always working behind the scenes, and He's working all things out for our good! My friends Payne and Shea were reassured in this way, and they stood firm in their faith from the start of the battle.

I was thrilled for Payne and Shea when they first fell in love after a mission trip together. They both served the Lord with all of their hearts. I couldn't wait for Payne to propose to my sweet friend because I knew she had already been praying for God to have His way. Payne, of course, had a great proposal planned. Payne knew Shea would have no suspicion of the proposal because he flew thousands of miles to surprise her. Together, in marriage, they are such an amazing team for God's Kingdom. Their love and faith in God shone even brighter in the fiery trial they faced.

After they married, Payne began to lose weight and have strange health complications. His family and friends began to wonder if something serious could be wrong. Unfortunately, they discovered Payne's liver was failing, but their faith was unwavering. I want you to be able to be stirred in your faith by their story:

> What is organ donation? Organ donation is many different things to many different people, but one thing it always is-HOPE.
>
> Organ donation is a young married couple receiving a diagnosis for which treatment will ultimately be transplant. It

is uncertainty and questions but steadfast confidence because of a mighty God and eternal hope. It is continuing on with life as normally as possible for as long as possible until impossible.

Organ donation is multiple hospital stays prior to transplant for the most random of ailments due to compromised immunity. It is fatigue and sickness and jaundice and too many more symptoms to list or even want to.

Organ donation is a slow decline until it is only sleepless nights and hoping for restful days on the couch at home. It is constant awareness of a phone call that has not come yet, but is hoped for in every passing moment.

Organ donation is staring death in the face every time you look in the mirror and wondering if it'll ever look familiar to you again. It is weight loss and severe muscle loss. It is losing the ability to do anything physical you ever loved— any sport or hobby you ever enjoyed. It is your body in a constant state of fighting. It is more medicine bottles than you ever imagined possible to prescribe to one human.

Organ donation is leaving your home less and less frequently because of weakness and risk of germ exposure. It is bottles upon bottles of germ-X and having to turn down precious visits from loved ones.

Organ donation is sitting on the couch with your spouse imagining together what it will be like to receive *that call*. It is finally receiving *that call* just to receive another one stating that it wasn't a good match after all. It is experiencing the greatest adrenaline rise and fall of your life and then picking your heart up and remembering that God is sovereign and in control.

Organ donation is hope.

Organ donation is receiving *the call. The call.* It is a teary-eyed, breath-held ride to the hospital, praying that this is the one. It is waivers and paperwork signed in a room waiting for the roll down the hallway that will change your life.

Organ donation is a long surgery. It is the greatest relief someone's spouse and family has ever felt just to touch their loved one after hours and to know they are smack dab in the moments they had been praying for.

Organ donation is a vast possibility of recovery processes. Everybody is different, and everyone's healing is different. Organ donation is teams and teams of doctors to care for the recipient post-transplant and set them up for physical success.

Organ donation is hope.

Organ donation is a young couple back doing what they love again—together. It is health and wholeness. It is stumbling blocks medically that will never defeat us after our God has given such victory, and He will continue to.

Organ donation is being mindful every single day of the fullness of health and life. It is obtaining perspective that we pray never clouds again.

Organ donation is moving *forward* in life finally to what lies ahead!

Organ donation is hope.

Organ donation is over a year post-surgery with twelve months full of progress and excitement for the future. It is prayerfully moving forward with jobs and plans and asking our sweet Savior for His timing in it all.

Organ donation is a letter to your donor's family, trying to adequately explain with pen and paper just what they have given. Hope, life, future, health, years and years and years, family, joy, enabling another mouthpiece to continue proclaiming the Gospel of Jesus! It is not receiving a letter back but hoping for the rest of your days that maybe they will write back, no matter how long they wait.

Organ donation is wondering forever who they were. Man or woman? What did they love? Where did they go? What were their passions? When did they decide to be an organ donor? Did they have *any idea* what they would mean to the person they chose to give life in the midst of inevitable death? The questions are absolutely endless.

Organ donation is hope—and so much more.

Organ donation is that young couple driving home on a rainy Thursday night with curious minds. It's finally getting home and getting an answer they have waited for for years.

Organ donation is a tiny plus sign on a little stick that changed their lives.

Organ donation is the moment of shock and thrill and exploding hearts that they had been asking God to have His way and timing in allowing.

Organ donation is a baby in our arms in July 2017, and it is all because of my husband's donor. Because of this person, my kids will have kids who will have kids who will have kids who will have kids, and so on. *Generations* were literally birthed when my husband's donor said, "Yes," whenever that was. Whether it was before a major surgery that took a turn for the worse, or at a DMV ten years before/thirty years before/two weeks before, there is no way to ever know.

Organ donation is us raising our baby starting this year and our babies in the years to come to know how sovereign and mighty and able our Jesus is. Our prayer is that they will grow up in love and enamored with our glorious King and be resounding voices for their generation declaring His Kingdom. Which means the people who come to know Jesus through our baby and our babies' babies, etc. will all be because of this *one donor who said, "Yes."*

Organ donation is a mind-blowing picture of how vast our God's reach is through us. He is all-powerful, almighty, ever-present, ever-loving, merciful beyond words, and gracious beyond our understanding, and He extended all of this through us in such a beautiful way through my husband's donor.

Organ donation is farther reaching than we can ever know. It is bringing life from inevitable death—but not just one life. It is bringing *generations* from inevitable death.

Organ donation is this wife praying that the reality of the *magnitude* of the gift we all hold in our precious bodies is realized. Your "yes" now, that little heart on your license, is full of more life and purpose than you could ever imagine.

Organ donation is our dream of becoming parents becoming reality in July 2017, and we could not be more *thankful* already for this little life! [12]

Not only are Payne and Shea parents now, but they have two children! Shortly after Shea became pregnant, God gave me a dream of their gender reveal. I saw a pink balloon first (Shea was pregnant with a girl at the time), and after a pause, I also saw a blue balloon (representing their second child). I am so grateful God fulfilled this dream in His perfect timing. Because of the miracle-working power of God displayed in Payne's life, an entire generation gets to know God's love!

Declarations

We can speak in faith. Faith is our "title deed." I love Hebrews 11:1 in the Amplified Bible. It says, "Now faith is the assurance (title deed, confirmation) of things hoped for (divinely guaranteed), and the evidence of things not seen [the conviction of their reality—faith comprehends as fact what cannot be experienced by the physical senses]." We have the title deed to what God has prepared for us. We don't have to let the enemy take from us. The promises in God's Word are for us! We take what God has for us by standing firmly on what He has spoken. When everything else around us says differently, we can speak what God says. We can ask the Lord for His will to be done on earth as it is in heaven.

There is power when we say what God says. It's important to declare His Word:

- **I can do all things through Christ, who strengthens me.** "Whatever I have, wherever I am, I can make it through anything in the One who makes me who I am." (Philippians 4:13 NKJV and MSG)
- **I am a new creation in Christ.** "Therefore, if anyone is in Christ, he is a new creation; old things have passed away; behold, all things have become new." (2 Corinthians 5:17 NKJV)
- **I have authority in Christ.** "I have given you authority to trample on snakes and scorpions and to overcome all the power of the enemy; nothing will harm you." (Luke 10:19 NKJV)
- **I am above only and not beneath.** "And the Lord will make you the head and not the tail; you shall be above only, and not be beneath, if you heed

the commandments of the Lord your God, which I command you today, and are careful to observe them." (Deuteronomy 28:13 NKJV)

- **I am more than a conqueror.** "Yet in all these things we are more than conquerors through Him who loved us." (Romans 8:37 NKJV)

Who does God say you are? Declare His promises.

God's Speciality

Yes, walking in faith can seem difficult sometimes, especially when you are believing for something big. But it's not impossible! Yes, it may be a stretch for human comprehension—that's why it's called a miracle (an event that appears to be contrary to the laws of nature and is regarded as an act of God—a mighty work). Miracles are God's specialty!

It's all right to acknowledge the struggle. This was something that I've come to realize more recently. It's always been hard for me to vocalize when things were tough. When I was in a lot of pain or stressed, I viewed even answering the question "How are you?" or "How are you feeling?" as negative if I told the details. But there are times when we need to be extremely transparent so that people can pray and help us.

Pain comes. Setbacks come. But in the midst of all things, God's word is still true. Make sure you elevate God's Word over your circumstance. When hard times come, the number-one goal of the enemy is to get you discouraged or disappointed. Yes, your situation is hard. You may be sick, dealing with financial trouble, or struggling with grief or loss. If you are feeling this way now, feeling down and experiencing trouble, know this: your perspective is key! Think from a place of knowing—this is not forever!

The next thing you need to know is that your environment needs to shift. Your environment has to be conducive for the harvest you desire. When farmers plant a seed, they are not thinking, *Well, I hope this works!* They know the principles surrounding seedtime and harvest. They know how to cultivate the environment necessary to produce a good harvest. We all must shift and cultivate the environment we need for harvest. If you're in a drought, you have to make sure you get water somehow. If you're experiencing a flood, more water is not what you need.

The same is true for us. Seedtime and harvest works. Do you need encouragement? Surround yourself with positivity and faith. Do you need blessing on your business? Give into good soil. Learn from others who have succeeded in what you are trying to do. Always have a teachable attitude. If you are teachable, you will learn. If you continue to learn, you will grow.

What do you need in this season? Cultivate that in your environment. When I need direction, I pray for God to show me the way. When I need peace, I pray the Psalms. When I need deliverance, I cry out to God. When I need help, I know He is my ever-present help. The answer to your need is a prayer away. Ask.

SIX

Obedience Is Big

Today you have [openly] declared the Lord to be your God, and that you will walk [that is, live each and every day] in His ways and keep His statutes, His commandments, and His judgments (precepts), and listen to His voice. Today the Lord has declared that you are His people, His treasured possession, just as He promised you, and that you are to keep all His commandments.

—Deuteronomy 26:17–18 (AMP)

Treasure

There's nothing you could do to earn more value. You are already treasured because God spoke it. You are not treasured because of any of your works. You are treasured because you belong to God.

From this place of belonging to God, our love's response is to keep all of His commandments. Because God loves us, and we love Him, we walk in obedience. Ruth, out of her love for Naomi, stayed close to her. In the same way, out of our love for God, we will want to stay close to Him.

Do you remember when we learned that Ruth is recorded as the first steadfast person in the Bible? She was obedient to go where she felt God leading her. Ruth didn't know the type of fruit that would come from her obedience. She just understood and believed that her reward was with God.

Obedience will always bear fruit. No matter what God asks you to do, your obedience will be fruitful. Ruth was able to birth greatness from her obedience. Her great grandchild was King David, and King David was a predecessor of Jesus!

Ruth and Naomi faced heartbreak and hard times. But God can turn any situation around. God choose to bring a new beginning from what looked like the end. God always brings beauty from ashes if we let Him. Will you let God bring fruit from the soil of your situation?

The Call

God is calling you today. He has put something inside of you that no one else has. Did you catch that? The world needs *you*. When you are called and commissioned, you are *anointed—chosen* for a particular thing. Imagine if David didn't answer the call He was anointed for. Imagine if Ruth didn't answer the call—the compelling of the Lord—to stay. In more modern times, imagine if Dr. Martin Luther King Jr. didn't answer the call to stand against racism and prejudice. History would be entirely different.

From the character and integrity in their hearts, they

all were obedient to answer the call. We will reap the benefits of their courage forever. We still need to follow in their footsteps of bravery today.

What's on your heart? What has God spoken? What do you dream about? What is the thing you can't shake? Could it be your call? Take courage today, treasured one. Only you can leave the mark you were called to make with your fingerprint on this world. Will you answer the call to imprint this world?

I'm not just talking about your natural fingerprints; I'm talking about what's inside of your spirit. It's time to awaken the deep purpose in you and walk in obedience. Are you ready to leave your mark? Are you ready to take steps in obedience? If so, those purposeful steps will lead to fruitfulness and fulfilled promises. Every step is an invitation for others to join you in walking in true purpose.

Some seasons of sowing are longer than others, but oh, when the harvest comes! It's far beyond any harvest you've seen before. The fruit is lasting. It's good, and it brings more joy than any difficult season. We won't lack any good thing when we seek the Lord and walk in righteousness (see Psalm 34:10 and 84:11).

Obedience reminds us that it's not about what we want. Obedience is about surrendering to what God wants. For example, I don't want to get up early. I don't want to have a busy schedule. But, ultimately, I will do things that push me to answer what God has called me to do. It's not about what I want. Obedience is about character. It's about righteousness. It's about pleasing God the Father and bringing heaven to earth.

Yielding

In Luke 11, Jesus's prayer shows us how to yield to the Father. Obedience is about yielding to God's will, but it also comes with the most amazing promise. If we learn to yield to His will, His will is established on earth as in Heaven. We can reap a heavenly harvest here on earth by sowing our obedience.

Active

Obedience is the way you make your faith active. It's how you move forward. Faith takes a step of obedience even when the outcome is unknown. Imagine if God opened a door for you. It would be rude or even oblivious of you not to walk through it! I believe obedience looks like various types of movement, and I believe faith and obedience walk through open doors.

In the Gospels, when I research Jesus's movement, I find that Jesus was motivated by one thing—compassion. Scripture says in the Gospels Matthew and Mark, "Jesus … moved with compassion."

Moved with Compassion

Jesus was moved by compassion for great deeds. With compassion, He:

- taught the people because they were like sheep with no shepherd (see Matthew 9:36 NKJV).

- healed the sick (see Matthew 14:14 NKJV).
- fed the hungry (see Matthew 15:32 NKJV).
- inspired others to forgive debts (see Matthew 18:27 NKJV).

We, too, should follow the lead of Jesus. We all need to be motivated by compassion. We need to be led by our love for one another. Jesus tells us in John 14:15 in The Passion Translation that "Loving me [Jesus] empowers you to obey my commands." Verses 15–17 are paraphrased in the MSG like this:

> If you love me, show it by doing what I've told you. I will talk to the Father, and he'll provide you another Friend so that you will always have someone with you. This Friend is the Spirit of Truth. The godless world can't take him in because it doesn't have eyes to see him, doesn't know what to look for. But you know him already because he has been staying with you, and will even be *in* you!

If we truly desire to walk in obedience, we also need to walk in love and empowerment, which are directly tied to compassion. Are you seeing how important compassion is in this journey? Compassion must be the driving force behind our obedience.

We must not obey *only* because it is in our best interests. We need to walk steadfast in our journey because *with compassion* we realize it's not all about us. This journey to answer God's call is so much bigger than us. It's about God, His plan, and ultimately His people. It's about others.

We need to realize how powerful obedience truly is. If we walk in obedience *with the help and empowerment of the Holy Spirit*, we can set a trail of obedience that generations to come can follow.

Walking in obedience to what you are called to do impacts countless lives. When you move in agreement with what you were created to do, multitudes will see the image of Whom you were created in. Many will see the glory of God!

His Glory

The impact of your obedience may seem small at first. But, in time, your seed of obedience grows into a harvest. Obeying your call reserves heavenly blessings for you. Obedience is your reservation for the things to come. Remember, obedience keeps your faith active. It puts value on the seeds you planted. Your obedience demonstrates that you understand there is endless potential in even the smallest seed. It shows that you believe your obedience is like an investment.

Investments

To some, investments seem risky. But those who know the ups and downs of the world market also know investments yield return. There is no greater rate of return than when investing in heaven's economy. When we invest in our future through obedience, our underwriter is God Almighty.

What is it that you feel called to do? Identify that, and then identify steps that you can take in obedience. Faith and wholehearted obedience to God's call rarely makes sense to this world. But obedience is currency in God's economy. Scripture shows us that God even sees faith as measurable.

What's the biggest dream inside your heart? Deep, deep down, what is it that your imagination would love to see happen? Is it ending world hunger? Is it having a family? Is it starting your own business? Whatever it is, whatever you long to do, I believe there are steps that you can take to walk closer to that reality.

Ask God, "What is one thing I can do to make room for this dream? God, what step of obedience are you asking me to take?" Whatever comes to your mind and spirit, write it down and do it. Take that step as an investment. The truth is, that small investment towards your dream makes room for your future. And, if you're having trouble imagining this—imagining investing and believing in a good future—know this:

> "God began a good work in you. And I am sure that he will carry it on until it is completed. That will be on the day Christ Jesus returns." (Philippians 1:6 NIRV)

"For I know the plans I have for you,'
declares the Lord, 'plans to prosper you
and not to harm you, plans to give you
hope and a future.'" (Jeremiah 29:11 NIV)

God has good plans for your life, friend. Strive to believe it before you see it. You will be amazed!

Practical Investments

When I first began dreaming about my future, I began prayer journaling. I would write down what I felt what God was speaking to me in our time together. That has proven to be one of the most special things I have done to invest in and believe in the future God has for me. Maybe starting a prayer journal is also a way for you to invest and believe in your future!

Another practical investment may be for you to create a vision board. If you are unsure of what a vision board is, I highly recommend researching it. Without vision, people and their dreams die. My vision board helps me envision my future and my goals. Intentionality is key to drawing closer to your vision. The corkboard where I pin my vision pictures helps me to make my vision plain.

I have photos on my vision board that represent this book surrounded by inspiring quotes, and I have a few photos of things I dream of checking off my bucket list. This year, I started accomplishing some of the dreams on the vision board, and so the top portion of the board is marked off for dreams achieved. When my dreams are realized, I move the photos above the mark of dreams achieved.

The funny thing is, I had a goal of going zip-lining pinned up on the vision board. More than zip-lining, though, I wanted to go skydiving, but I just didn't think that was realistic. I didn't imagine that I would ever get to go. But, one Summer day, I was scheduled to go zip-lining. But once I realized all the climbing and platforms involved in zip-lining, I decided to switch my activity that day. I went on a skydiving adventure instead! Can you believe it? All the limits I was familiar with on the ground flew away in the sky. The sky was no longer the limit!

Would you believe me if I said the sky is not the limit for you? Your sky has no limit! Will you allow yourself to push past the limitations you place on yourself? Let yourself flourish! Don't stifle yourself because you're not sure what type of fruit will come from taking steps of faith.

Obedience means you know what God has asked of you. It means you seek the Lord, know Him, and love Him.

> The young lions lack and suffer hunger;
> But those who seek the Lord shall not
> lack any good thing.
> —Psalm 34:10 (NKJV)

Activate

Remember how obedience keeps your faith active? Obedience puts faith into motion, but it also activates something greater. Obedience activates your promise.

It's time to experience your miracle. It's time to run with the promises of God. It's time to shift and move into another land—another dimension. If you can only catch the vision and apply obedience, you will know the promise is yours for the taking.

It's time for you to go beyond dreaming about your promise. It's time for you to experience walking into it! Don't just get close to it. Don't get to the border of promise and be satisfied. God has more for you. It's here. God delights in giving you the promise. He delights not because you seek it but because you seek Him.

Are you ready for your life to be an astounding testimony of the love and power of God? Obedience isn't your ticket to get whatever you want from the Father. It's your way of showing Abba that you believe Him and you love Him with your whole heart. It demonstrates that you know God is up to something and that you desperately desire to be a part of it!

Just like Ruth, you can choose to sow seeds of obedience, believing they will yield fruit.

SEVEN

Walk in Love

But God shows and clearly proves His [own] love
for us by the fact that while we were still sinners,
Christ (the Messiah, the Anointed One) died for us.

—Romans 5:8 (AMPC)

Up until this point, the journey toward the promise has been all uphill. It's like we've been ascending a mountain. The climb has not been easy, and it seems long. But, our journey reaches a turn here. Along the journey so far, we've remained steadfast, we've built and trained our spirit, we've held fast, we've rejoiced, and we've stayed in faith and obedience. However, the next part of our journey is not about our steadfast walk anymore.

Now we've reached the top of our climb, but the summit is only the midpoint in our journey. Now there is a turn that we are going to take that changes our perspective. This turn shows us (especially me) that the process is not all about the climb itself. It's not always about reaching the next goal or the promise. It's about how our journey leads us closer to God and impacts others.

As I prepared to write about God's love, I was apprehensive and unsure of what was still ahead. To be honest, I was facing fear. I didn't expect to be learning as much as I have while writing this book. I thought I was familiar with the love of God. But love is better grasped through experience than through study.

Growing up, I clung to the Word of God. I studied it. I memorized it. I thought I knew some of the answers. I thought I understood God's nature. But, really, I didn't understand much. I just trusted in my favorite verse, Psalm 46:1: "God is our refuge and strength, an ever-present help in trouble" (NIV).

Without His ever-present help, I wouldn't have made it this far. The climb would have been too difficult if not for His strength. But I've never taken this turn into the *depth* of God's love before. This turn in the road requires me to face and abandon all my fears if I want to encounter perfect love (see 1 John 4:18).

As I stared down my fears, God's love whispered something I never expected to hear in a million years. Scared, praying on the edge of worry and frustration, I heard the whisper: "We want the same things. Trust me." Could this be true? Is what I am praying for what God wants for me, too? In that moment, fear, worry, and frustration melted away.

You may think that wanting "the same things" as God is far-fetched. How can our human minds decipher His holy will? But, I believe if our number-one priority is the fear of the Lord and staying close to Him, we won't want to do anything that would draw us away from Him. Can you confidently say, "God and I want the same things, and I just need to trust Him"?

I believe you will be able to after you encounter Him and His nature! It's His love and compassion that made a way for us to know Him. It is His unending love that died for us. We have to know His love to know Him fully. I want to step into a place where I know His love even more intimately. I don't want to become numb to it; I want to experience it in a fresh way every day.

It felt like a long time passed before I could even write this chapter. God's mercies and His love are new every morning (see Lamentations 3:22–23). Yet, at the same time, He's unchanging—He's the same yesterday, today, and forever (see Hebrews 13:8), and His love never ceases. There is no love more steadfast than His love. It's so great that it's hard to put into words.

In my weakness, I constantly have ups and downs. But, as I encounter God's love, He covers my weakness. He covers all my errors, faults, and sins. His love makes me stronger. God's love shows me His heart. It shows me His character. It puts me at ease and rests any place of striving in me. In my own strength, I have come as far as I can on this journey. Now there is nowhere to turn but to Him.

Oh, what a good thing this fork in the road is! There is no good thing in me apart from Him. When I have no strength left in me, His love casts out all of my fear. His love is able to cover me at all times and take over. At this point in the journey, I am no longer in the valley, and I'm not climbing, either. I've taken a rest to be with Him.

A Vision of High Places

I had a vision that the Lord set a table before me. Everything in me felt unworthy I thought, *What have I done to deserve this? There's a table that could be set for at least a dozen, and yet it's just me and Jesus. We're in the heights, and He is waiting for me to sit down with Him. Lord, shouldn't I go and bring others to the table? What do you want me to do, God? There are other seats at this table. This can't just be for me.*

Unwavering, He still waited for me to sit in His presence. I knew I was to take my place at the table. As I went to sit down and learn from Him, there were others who lived in the heights that came to sit down. I had the sense that they had eaten at this table before. They knew the Lord's love intimately, but now the Lord invited me—just as He wants to invite all of us—to know His love so that we may know Him fully (see Ephesians 3:19).

At the table, there was fruit in front of us. It was vibrant with color and satisfying. We began feasting on His fruit. It was unlike any fruit I had tasted, because we were eating the fruit of Who He is.

His love.

His joy.

His peace.

His patience.

His kindness.

His goodness.

His faithfulness.

His gentleness.

His temperance.

Each one of us at the table became full, but not just of fruit—we were full of Him. With every bite we took, we experienced Him. We knew Him because we sat with Him. We learned from Him. We ate from His table. But, more than that, we ate of the revelation of Who He is.

In His presence, there is the fruit of the Spirit (see Galatians 5:22–23).

Every good thing comes from Him. Any good fruit we see in our lives is not a by-product of our works. It's from Him. Every good thing in us is from Him. He so richly loves us that He offers the best fruits for us. In His presence, there is no lack. He is everything we need.

When was the last time you sat with Him? When is the last time you were filled with Him to overflowing? We have to eat of His fruit before it can overflow in our lives. Abide in Him. Feast on His love. His joy. His peace! When you feast on this fruit till overflowing, others will see fruit in you! They will see your love for one another. They will encounter *Jesus* through you.

This is why it is so important to *abide* in Him—to *know* Him. Apart from Him, we can do nothing! There is no fruitfulness without Him. This point in the journey is *life-changing* for *others*. When you truly encounter *Jesus*, others will encounter *Jesus* through you.

— EIGHT —

Unrelenting Grace

But He said to me, "My grace is sufficient for
you, for my power is made perfect in weakness."
Therefore I will boast all the more gladly about my
weaknesses, so that Christ's power may rest on me.

—2 Corinthians 12:9 (NIV)

I know that I'm weak. My weakness is glaringly obvious, and because of it, I cannot gain any ground on my own. It's the partnership with God's strength that makes all the difference. This partnership is made possible by grace. Grace is the divine influence upon your heart that empowers you. It is a supernatural force. This force is why I am able to confidently say, "My weakness *is* enough. It's perfect to partner with God's strength."

God is on my side. I don't have to beg for His grace. He actually wants me to boast in my weakness. I'm still learning to do this, but the more I do it, the more I see His sufficiency. He carries me, and shows Himself strong in the midst of my weakness. I boast that I *can't* because He *can*! He always delights in making the impossible possible. He always causes us to triumph (see 2 Corinthians 2:14).

His grace empowers us to come to His throne. And at His throne, Heaven can meet earth.

> For we do not have a high priest who is unable to empathize with our weaknesses, but we have one who has been tempted in every way, just as we are—yet he did not sin. Let us then approach God's throne of grace with confidence, so that we may receive mercy and find grace to help us in our time of need. (Hebrews 4:15–16 NIV)

His grace emboldens us with the power of heaven. We do not have to settle for the confines of this life. We can call out for help and expect an answer. God's grace abounds to meet all of our needs (see 2 Corinthians 9:8). This means that God's grace can overshadow any area of lack in our lives.

As I was feasting in the high places, I knew I didn't do anything to earn a seat at the table. God's love and grace just make a way for us. His love abounds so greatly, and His grace is a deep well that never runs out. It's available to everyone. Once we taste of it, we can run and tell others.

I'm ready to run. I'm ready to shout, "You are seen, you are loved, and you have a seat at the King's table!"

There is a roar in me now that started as a whisper. It simply started by realizing that I have a place at the King's table. Let me tell you: you're invited. Don't wait. Don't change clothes. Don't try to earn the free invitation of grace. The time for grace is now. Just accept the invitation. Come as you are. Taste and see that the Lord is good.

If you could see the invitation, you would see it is addressed to you—no mistake. It is pure evidence of grace. We didn't earn it, but we have access to it. Will you accept the invitation?

If you're ready, let's go to the high places. Let's move forward. Let's move higher.

Giving Yourself Grace

Now that you're aware of your place at the table, don't disqualify yourself from this high place. Don't convince yourself of why you don't deserve the grace and love of God. You'll never win that game, because grace is a gift. It's freely given. It's okay to feel inadequate and humbly grateful. If you want to express to the Lord how grateful you are for grace, try boasting in your weakness and in His strength. Be joyful in it. Acknowledge that God is with you, empowering you in the steps you take each day.

When I don't boast in my weakness well, I sometimes feel guilty for giving myself grace. Have you ever put yourself down for your weakness? I'm assuming we all have, right? When the enemy tries to bring you down and shame you in this way, I challenge you to give yourself more grace. Boast in God's strength, which will help you overcome whatever you're walking through. His strong hand is sure to hold you up.

One day in particular when I was putting myself down, I heard the Lord bring encouragement and clarity. These words pierced through my heart: "If it's something I'm asking you to do, I want you to have the courage to do it. If it's not something I'm asking you to do, then don't worry about it." Wow. Worry and guilt can come in when we're thinking on too many things. Here I was thinking about all the areas in my life that I wasn't acing, while all God wanted was for me to follow Him and be courageous where He led me. In other words, if it's not essential, don't let it take over your mind. Give yourself grace for all things, but know how to focus on the main thing. Our works don't make us fruitful; being close to the vine does. That's the main thing (see John 15:5).

Taking Your Seat

God's grace and favor reserves your spot at His table. When I go to a restaurant, I don't sit at a stranger's table. I go where I'm invited to sit and dine. Typically, I sit with those I'm close to. We share food, love, and laughter. (I'm usually the one laughing so much it hurts.)

We have an invitation to sit and dwell with the King of kings. He wants us close to Him. Let's not shy away from special moments with Him. Once you take your seat, you'll know that's where you belong. And, you'll realize the table is big enough for the entire Kingdom—so you can invite others to come to the table, too.

Favor

If you're already aware of this invitation to come to the table, or if you have already taken your seat, I'm sure you know this, too:

You have favor with God. He paid the highest price for you.

It's humbling, but there is no other explanation. We are found blameless in God's sight when we are covered in the blood of Christ. Grace and favor often come from the same Hebrew word in scripture. They're both undeserved and freely given. It's our inheritance. Our human name is not our identity. Our identity is son or daughter of God. You are who God says you are—you are His.

Belonging to the family of God inherently means you are royal. And favor follows royalty! Just like in the parable of the prodigal son, everything the Father has also belongs to the children (see Luke 15:31). Favor, just like grace, cannot be earned; it is given. It gives you access to undeserved benefits. As a child of God, you have access. God has already given His children the keys to the Kingdom. This means we can we can unlock heaven on earth now! Why wait until heaven to use your keys? We'll already be in the gates. Steward your keys and your gifts here and now.

Keys make me think of open doors. Did you know

there are storehouses in heaven? Supposedly that's where the snow and rain is held (Job 38:22). But I think there are storehouses that contain our blessings, too. They're probably filled with things with our names on them. Every blessing comes down from above, and God can't wait to give them to you. He's already given you the keys. He wants you to unlock heaven's resources now. You see, grace and favor gives you access to everything you need to fulfill the God-given assignment on your life.

Have you ever searched for something that was right under your nose? Sometimes I dig and dig through my purse and still can't seem to find what I'm looking for. Usually, it's my phone or a small item. I keep digging because I know it's in there. It's only a matter of time before all that digging pays off. That's what it feels like I'm doing in this season of life—writing this book— digging for something I know is there. And, if I don't give up, I'll discover what has been there all along. God's already given you what you need, too. Keep digging.

The weight of favor can break chains and set you free from bondage.

Favor was given to the Israelites in the sight of the Egyptians to let them go from captivity (Exodus 12:36). Favor was given to Joseph while captive in prison. "But the Lord was with Joseph and showed him mercy, and He gave him favor in the sight of the keeper of the prison" (Genesis 39:21 NKJV). After this, God gave Joseph favor in the sight of Pharaoh, and he was put in charge of the entire land of Egypt (Genesis 41:40–41)! Did you catch that? God's kind of favor can set you free *and* put you in charge!

Favor will bring you from a low place to a higher place. Favor presents you with opportunities to draw out the greatness God has put inside of you. It places you in the presence of the great. But, again, this place of favor has purpose. Those with favor have been entrusted with authority. Are you stewarding this responsibility well?

Favor is not given to build up one person. It is given for the advancement of the Kingdom of God. It's not too extravagant. It always has purpose. Let God lavish His love and favor on you.

There are no limits to what God can do. There are no limits to His love, grace, and favor. He has unlimited resources, and we have access to all of them.

> So I kneel humbly in awe before the Father of our Lord Jesus, the Messiah, the perfect Father of every father and child in heaven and on the earth. And I pray that he would unveil within you the unlimited riches of his glory and favor until supernatural strength floods your innermost being with his divine might and explosive power. Then, by constantly using your faith, the life of Christ will be released deep inside you, and the resting place of his love will become the very source and root of your life. (Ephesians 3:14–17 TPT)

If you're doing God's Kingdom work, all of heaven is behind you. You have the best investors because God orders His angels to listen for His word and do it (see Psalm 103:20). Once you grasp that you are empowered by grace, and you are not alone in this battle, you will move forward knowing nothing is too hard for God!

Ascending the Heights

I pray the Lord opens your eyes to see His mighty hand that is holding you steady every step of your journey. As God would have it, I got to go to the mountains soon after comparing this journey to climbing a mountain. I decided to attempt hiking for the first time! As I was ascending this incline—actually, as I was trying to make it to the base of the incline, I thought I was going to have to surrender my dream before even starting. *I barely made it up the hill to the start of the incline,* I thought, *but I've got to try. Don't be hard on yourself. Even if your best is five steps, be proud of your attempt, because if you face the impossible, it gives other people permission to do the same.*

So, slowly, I started up the incline of this mountain. With my mom on one side and my new God-sent angel of a friend, Jessi, on the other, I took a firm grip on the dream to hike up this mountain.

Yes, I know walking is a miracle for me. It was probably dangerous for me to go up these incline stairs, but I had a certainty in my heart that God was inviting me to experience more of Him with every step. Before I knew it, I had surpassed five, ten, and twenty steps, and my friend Jessi saw our first marker—one hundred steps. "What? Let's keep going to two hundred!" We made it to two hundred. "Do you think we can make it to 320? I want to make it to 320 for Ephesians 3:20!" I said.

Once we made it to 320, I had to stop for a photo to capture the amazing moment! I was so happy, and God's supernatural strength was evident. I wanted to keep going. Once I made it to four hundred, my desire was to make it to five hundred steps. But, my mom, being more realistic, said that it was time to turn back. The incline was continuing to get steeper with every step, and we still had to think about getting back down.

"I just want to make it to five hundred. Please?" I asked.

"No," Mom said as a voice of reason. "Well, wait," she said, seeing potential help on the way. "Let's see what happens."

"Can't stop, won't stop," came the voice of one man's encouragement to keep going.

"Are you going to help?" I asked.

"She wants to make it to five hundred," said my mom.

"Sure. Let's go!" he said.

My feet weren't the steadiest along the way. My mom pointed out that my legs were shaking as we began ascending again. But I had a sturdy helping hand. When I slipped, my encourager reassured me, "I've got you." And I made it to five hundred steps with his help! I didn't feel judged for my slow progress; I felt celebrated as others began to cheer, knowing I reached my summit!

Isn't that the way God equips and encourages us? He gives us His strong hand, and celebrates each slow and steady step of progress like it's the summit! His grace empowers us to keep going. We continue discovering that in our weakness, He makes us strong. It's God's mercies that are new every morning. Because of this, we don't have to stay where we are today. We can reach new heights!

Do you have the courage to step into more of what God has for you? I promise He's got you!

PART THREE

Entering The Promise Land

— NINE —

Immeasurably More

Now to him who is able to do immeasurably more than all we ask or imagine, according to his power that is at work within us, to him be glory in the church and in Christ Jesus throughout all generations, for ever and ever! Amen."

—Ephesians 3:20-21 (NIV)

Along my journey up the mountain incline, I learned a new term. Did you know there's something called a "false summit"? It's what appears to be the top of the mountain, and yet it's not the tip-top. Somehow, in my heart, I knew that anything less than five hundred steps would be my false summit this time. (Next time, I'll reach the top!)

Once we reached five hundred steps and the cheers died down, there was a rock that became a perfect seat for me. I was just soaking in this moment as much as I could. I was in awe!

What would have happened if I had stopped short

of what was in my heart? I believe I would have only seen a small glimpse of who God is and what He has for me. Every glimpse is meaningful, of course, but it's important we see from a higher perspective. Sitting on that rock that day represented where I truly sit—in heavenly places.

> And God raised us up with Christ and seated us with him in the heavenly realms in Christ Jesus, in order that in the coming ages he might show the incomparable riches of his grace, expressed in his kindness to us in Christ Jesus. (Ephesians 2:6–7 NIV)

If you see with heaven's perspective, you know that you're seated far above any circumstance or problem. Even what feels like the biggest mountain in your way is just a tiny hill from heaven's viewpoint. Imagine looking down at every problem from the perspective of an airplane window.

We're just specks on this earth, and yet God knows our names. He created us in His image with purpose. He loves us so much that He offers us new life in Christ. How awesome is that? It seems wild, but it's not outlandish or too good to be true. It's reality. God eagerly waits for us to call out to Him. And He is there.

I imagined that the ascent of this incline represented a huge victory for me, and it did! I discovered a great and simple truth through my experience: God has carried me to every summit in my life. God is the One who carries us. He's not just in the high places. God is present in every low place *and* at every summit. You don't have to make it to the top of your mountain to see Him in a grand way. It's grand knowing He is *with us* every step of the way. No matter we are in our journey, God is *with us*! But don't let that keep you comfortable staying in the same place.

There is immeasurably more to life with Him than you could ever imagine. Don't stop when you reach a false summit. Stay in awe and wonder. Keep going! Stand on the next promise. Discover the next triumph. And, just when you think you've reached the top, God is there to carry you higher!

Don't think too small. Always seek God's perspective. The victories you see in your lifetime will have an impact and leave a legacy for generations to come!

Steadfast one, you will run with the promises of God when you trust Him! Let Him carry you higher and show you more than you ever thought possible. There are no limits for us who live in heaven's reality. God always responds to our faith.

Let me tell you, instead of having an irreversible disability, I have irreversible hope. There's nothing my God cannot do, and there is no good thing He withholds from me. My God promises I will run and not grow weary. If God says I can have it, it's mine! And, God says we can have it, so it's ours! Now that we've taken this *Walk Steadfast* journey, who wants to run with me? I've got my running shoes, and I know we will never run out of hope!

For God has proved his love by giving us his greatest treasure, the gift of his Son. And since God freely offered him up as the sacrifice for us all, he certainly won't withhold from us anything else he has to give. (Romans 8:32 TPT)

Closing Prayer

I know you are about to arise and show your tender love to Zion. Now is the time, Lord, for your compassion and mercy to be poured out—the appointed time has come for your prophetic promises to be fulfilled!

—Psalm 102:13 (TPT)

Father God, thank you for giving us irreversible hope. The time has come for us to see your promises fulfilled. I ask that you would cover each one of us with your presence. Lead and guide us on our journeys. Let us see more of You than we ever dreamed. May we walk confidently in your strength every day and run boldly into your promises! All the glory is yours! We love you. Amen.

NOTES

1   Batterson, Mark, *The Circle Maker*, p. 11.

2   Fulghum, Robert, *All I Really Need to Know I Learned in Kindergarten*, New York City, NY: Random House, 1986.

3   http://www.eliyah.com/cgi-bin/strongs.cgi?file=hebrewlexicon&isindex=3557

4   https://www.dictionary.com/browse/stability

5   5 https://www.apa.org/helpcenter/willpower-harnessing

6   https://www.childrenshospital.org/Centers-and-Services/Programs/A- -E/cerebral-palsy-program/what-is-cerebral-palsy

7   Lewis, C. S., *The Lion, the Witch and the Wardrobe* (New York City, NY: HarperCollins Publishers, 2001), 146.

8   Stead, M. R. Louisa, 'Tis So Sweet to Trust in Jesus, 1882.

9   https://youtu.be/Si4Dn5MYwWk

10 Walker, Hezekiah, "Every Praise," RCA Inspiration, October 17, 2013, video, 5:28, https://www.youtube.com/watch?v=UuuZMg6NVeA.

11 Capra, Frank, dir. *It's a Wonderful Life* Liberty Films, 1946

12 https://sheastockard.wordpress.com/2017/01/17/what-is-organ-donation/

Printed in the United States
By Bookmasters